A Histc

SALE

from earliest times to the present-day

N.V. SWAIN

First published in 1987 by
Sigma Press, 1 South Oak Lane, Wilmslow, Cheshire SK9 6AR, England.

Reprinted 1994.

ISBN 1 85058 086 3

British Library Cataloguing in Publication Data
 Swain, N.V.
 The history of Sale.
 1. Sale (Cheshire)--History
 I. Title
 942.7'31   DA690.S156/

Cover © *Airviews (Manchester) Ltd*
The aerial photograph of Sale town centre was taken in March, 1975. School Road is on the extreme right of the picture with the canal near the bottom passing beneath Sale Bridge. The main road is running across the picture towards the top.

Until the 19th century, what is now Sale town centre was practically devoid of buildings. For as far as the main road it was part of the common called Sale Moor until 1805, and only started to develop after the opening of the railway in 1849 – the station being named Sale Moor station until 1856.

Printed and bound by: Manchester Free Press.

ACKNOWLEDGEMENT

I wish to acknowledge my gratitude to Mr. Peter Lee for his kindness in loaning me copies of maps and schedules.

Foreword

At the end of my *Introduction to the History of Sale* which Sale Borough Council published a little over twenty years ago, I wrote that a fuller and more detailed work on Sale would undoubtedly be produced in the future, not at the time being certain that it would fall to myself to write it. However, circumstances in recent years having provided me with the necessary time, I took on the task, which was to produce a local history suitable both for schools and the general reader with an interest in Sale's past.

The first chapter sets out to show, from the evidence of field-names, that there was settlement in Sale during the late Anglo-Saxon period and also the type of farming which took place here later in the Middle Ages. For this purpose I have not relied on J. McNeal Dodgson's *Place-Names of Cheshire* because there are important field-names which Dodgson missed in the section on Sale; the reason being that he used the Sale Tithe Award of 1844 rather than the Enclosure Award of 1807. During the intervening years between the two sources some field-names changed and others were lost altogether.

For example, by 1844, Farry Yort had changed to Fairy Yard, Great and Little Tunacliffe Meadow had become Great Meadow, Nearer and Back Moor Fields had changed to the meaningless Big and Little Boggart Fields. For the Anglo-Saxon field-names I have used the abbreviation A.S. rather than the more modern O.E. for Old English, in order that there will be no doubt regarding the period under discussion.

Photographs in this book show various buildings in Sale and reference is sometimes made to a particular brick bond. Building a brick wall so that the vertical joints do not coincide is called bonding. When a brick is laid with the length visible it is called a stretcher; when the end of the brick is visible it is called a header. At first, building with brick in England did not conform to any recognisable bond, but in the Tudor period Old English bond was commonly used, this consisted of alternate courses of stretchers and headers. The earliest brick building surviving in Sale is nos. 118–120 Cross Street, dating from the late 17th century; this building is constructed of 2½″ (65 mm) thick bricks in modified English bond, commonly known as garden wall bond. Modified English bond consists of three to five courses of stretchers to one course of headers and, in Sale, it was used for many rural buildings before and after the construction of the railway.

During the 18th century, the more decorative Flemish bond appeared in this country and was used on Sale's rural buildings alongside modified English bond from at least 1800, Ashton New Hall being one early example. Flemish bond is alternate stretchers and headers in each course. The urban, post-railway, "villas" were for the most part constructed in stretcher bond which is, of course, stretchers only, and during the second half of the 19th century urban buildings in Sale including not only houses, but also the Sale Hotel, the police station and St. Martin's school, were wholly or partly built in header bond, that is, the ends of the bricks visible.

The photographs except where otherwise stated were taken during 1984-6 and include examples of various styles of domestic architecture to be found in Sale, both rural and urban; Sale's urban period of building beginning in the 1850s, the earlier rural period overlapping and lasting perhaps until about 1870 with vernacular buildings still being erected until then. Two buildings, not illustrated, were examples of houses in Sale following high fashion yet pre-dating the urban villas of the mid-Victorian perod in Sale. They were Sale Lodge, now the Golf Clubhouse, and Sale Old Hall. The former building, erected during the 1830s, is an example of the smaller Regency country house in the Classical tradition. Sale Old Hall, built a few years later, was a quite early representation of the Gothic Revival of Victoria's reign.

To conclude this foreword I would say that although my main interest is history I do not think that the past should be regarded with undue sentiment. There were never any such times as the "good old days" for life was hard centuries ago and ordinary people today have an infinitely higher standard of life than the wealthiest of the Middle Ages, higher technology bringing immense advances in agriculture, medicine and countless other fields and leading to the creation of a wealth of new products on a vast scale, all of which has immeasurably advanced the well-being of people; and, after all, technical progress is what, fundamentally, history is about.

N. V. Swain
Sale 1987

Norman Swain died in November 1992, but this book is a lasting tribute to a remarkable local historian. His original research material is in Sale Library where a room, which houses the collection, has been named after him.

Contents

List of Figures

To Averil, my wife.

1

The Beginnings of Sale

Sale is situated partly in the Mersey valley but, for the most part, just on the edge of the valley. Dane Road and Glebelands Road mark the southern edge of the valley in this area and Edge Lane, Stretford, the northern edge; all of Sale being less than 100ft. (30 metres) above sea level.

The area of the Mersey valley, from prehistoric times, formed an important route connecting the coast with the Pennines. Prehistoric man arrived in what is now Cheshire more than 6,000 years ago, preferring to live in hill-forts rather than on the plain; the only prehistoric find in Sale, so far as I am aware, being a flint arrow-head discovered in the sand layer in a garden in Holly Bank in 1894.

The Romans, as they conquered Britain, (the name Britain being derived from the Celtic inhabitants, the Pritani) constructed forts and roads linking them. The A56 through Sale is on the line of a Roman road which branched off Watling Street and connected the forts at Chester, Northwich and Manchester. Near West Timperley the modern road leaves the line of the Roman one, passes through Altrincham and rejoins the original route again.

In an area in this "gap" in 1965, pupils of North Cestrian Grammar School, under the direction of their history master Mr. C. D. Rogers, made several excavations and uncovered the cobbled surface of the Roman road. According to a report in the Sale and Stretford Guardian in 1938, blocks of sandstone measuring 4ft. (1.2 metres) × 1ft. (305mm) square were unearthed on the main road at a depth of 7ft. 8ins. (2.3 metres) a short distance from Timperley Brook; these may have been the remains of a Roman ford over the brook.

During the 18th century a rather curious incident occurred concerning the Roman period in this area; a scholarly hoax was perpetrated by Charles Bertram who was born in 1723. Bertram was fascinated by the Roman period to the extent that he, on occasions, signed himself Charles Julius. Charles's father moved with his family to Copenhagen, where the son obtained the post of English teacher in the school for naval cadets. At the age of 24 he conceived the idea of bringing himself into notice by means of a literary forgery.

In June, 1747 Bertram began a correspondence with Dr. William Stukeley, the antiquarian, in the course of which he mentioned that a friend of his was in possession of a manuscript work by Richard of Cirencester, who had been a monk of St. Peter's, Westminster in 1355; this included a copy of an ancient itinerary of Britain which, in reality, Charles Bertram had forged.

Stukeley read a paper to the Society of Antiquaries containing an analysis of the work, which was accepted as genuine, and later published. Bertram's forgery was conclusively exposed in the 1860s by B. B. Woodward the librarian of Windsor Castle.

In 1771, the Rev. John Whitaker published the first history of Manchester and used, as some of his source material, Stukeley's paper. This referred to a supposed Roman station called *Fines Maximae & Flaviae* located near the river Mersey. Whitaker decided that the site was in Ashton at the junction of Cross Street and what is now Glebelands Road or, as he describes it, "it was placed on the southerly side of the Mersey, on the right-hand side of the road and about musketshot from the bridge". Needless to say, no trace of a Roman structure has ever been found on the site; although the name of the station appeared on the first Ordnance Survey map of this area.

The history of Roman Britain has, of course, little relevance to the history of the English; for the early English, or Anglo-Saxons as they are usually called, did not arrive here until the end of the Roman occupation of Britain. The Germanic tribes to which the English belonged were never conquered by the Romans and, in fact, it was some of the Germanic tribes that brought about the final downfall of Rome.

Nothing survives here of the Roman occupation apart from a few ruins and roads – no language, no laws nor customs; the social fabric which the Britons inherited from the Romans was completely swept away by the arrival of the English, beginning in the fifth century.

The history of the English before that time would have to be sought between the North Sea and the Baltic in places like Schleswig and Jutland, for that is the area the English occupied before some of them settled in Britain. Their arrival here is usually referred to as English immigration; not an entirely adequate term as an immigrant is a person who exchanges his homeland for another, accepting the laws and customs which he finds there and becoming a subject of that state.

The English, generally speaking, have always been colonists, a far different thing; wherever they settled in the world they, sooner or later, imposed their own laws and customs and their language in many cases, to the extent that today English is the international language. Virtually all the English in modern times who could properly be described as immigrants went to countries which had already been colonised by their own people several generations before.

And so the early English who arrived in Britain were colonists and began setting up their settlements, clearing woodland and bringing land into cultivation. The Anglo-Saxons as the early English are called were, as everyone knows, comprised mainly of three tribes, the Angles, Saxons and Jutes, although there were also a few **Frisians**, Franks and others.

In their old homelands the Saxons were the southernmost of the three main tribes and lived to the north of what is now Bremen. The Angles occupied an area around Schleswig which was formerly called England, the place-name "England" still surviving in a small area there. The Jutes lived further north in what is still called Jutland in central Denmark.

They all spoke Old English, as Anglo-Saxon is now called, but with different dialects; hence the reason for the differing regional accents in England today; the accents of northern England being a legacy of our Anglian or, later, Danish and Norse ancestors.

After the English invasion of Britain, the Angles occupied a huge area of the eastern part of the country as far south as what was later to be Suffolk (the south folk), and by the time they pushed westward to colonise what is now Cheshire, probably not before the 7th century, they were Angles who had never seen their Continental place of origin, as they were several generations removed from the original colonisers. These people created the kingdom of Mercia which became an earldom when the kingdom of England was formed under Egbert in A.D. 829; the earldom being divided into shires, of which Chester shire or Cheshire was one, about A.D. 900. Although Cheshire was mainly occupied by Angles there was, later, Norse occupation around Wirral and some Danish occupation in east Cheshire.

We know that Sale existed as a settlement in the early Middle Ages because of a deed referring to a grant of land in "the township of Sale" in the 12th century. But, more importantly, because the deed refers to Sale as a township rather than a manor then, the inference is, there was a settlement in Sale during the Anglo-Saxon period.

The townships were an Anglo-Saxon creation and, although they existed as part of a feudal society, were a more democratic structure than the Norman manors which were eventually to supplant them; for, under the Normans, feudalism in England became more highly organised as the policy of *null terre sans seigneur* (no land without a lord) was embarked upon.

From this it follows that any township which existed after the Norman Conquest had also existed before the Conquest and would, sooner or later, become a Norman manor or part of one. If, as in the case of Sale, a century seems rather a long time for the township to have lingered on, the explanation must be sought in the events which followed the Norman Conquest of 1066.

There were a number of rebellions against Norman rule in 1068, including one in Mercia; in reply William laid waste the counties of York and Durham in 1069. A second rebellion occurred in Mercia and, in the mid-winter of 1069–70, William marched his army over the Pennines and it was Cheshire's turn to suffer devastation. It took a very long time for Cheshire to recover and, as it became a principal base in the wars with the Welsh over the following two centuries, emphasis was placed on keeping control and building up military strength; economic development, consequently, took second place.

Sale and Ashton are not mentioned in Domesday, but neither are many other places which are known to have existed at the time of the Conquest. The place-name "Sale" is considered by Ekwall in his *Dictionary of English Place-Names* to be derived from the Anglo-Saxon *sealh*, a willow; in other words the place where the willows grew and it is, presumably, on the basis of this that Dr. Dorothy Sylvester includes Sale in her Cheshire Atlas as an Anglo-Saxon settlement; but there is also the evidence of field and other names.

One of the most useful sources of information on Sale is the Sale Moor Enclosure Act of 1805, with which we shall deal in some detail later. When the Act had been passed a map of the whole of Sale was drawn the following year, along with a schedule which enables us to see the location of every field in the township, its size, shape and name, whether it was enclosed or not and the name of the owner. This is not only of value to us in seeing what Sale was like 180 years ago, but also enables us to build a picture of Sale in the Middle Ages. Firstly, the Anglo-Saxon names.

The most obvious is in the name of Dane Road; apart from the main road (A56) which is Roman in origin, Dane Road is probably the oldest road in Sale (Anglo-Saxon *denu, dene, daenland* – a valley). Dane Road runs along the edge of the Mersey valley. Deansgate in Manchester which skirts the Irwell valley has a similar derivation. Another road in Sale of probable Anglo-Saxon origin is Fairy Lane, almost a continuation of Dane Road (A.S. *faer*-road, way).

Field-names include Street Field which is located against the A56 near Crossford Bridge; this is unquestionably of Anglo-Saxon origin; street or *straet* being the name they gave to Roman roads. There are hursts (A.S. *hyrst* – a wood), a field near Crossford Bridge called Farry Yort (A.S. *feorr* – far; *eort* – earth or ground); Bettenshaw (A.S. *beteon*-enclose) and, returning to Dane Road, part of the road where the house called the Priory formerly stood is referred to in a court action of 1779 as Pataker Lane. Pataker will be a field-name which disappeared when the "Priory" was built (*paet* was late Northumbrian A.S. for valley); the Mersey being finally the boundary between Northumbria and Mercia; the name Mersey being derived from *mear* – boundary and *ea* – river.

Finally, an interesting field-name is great and little Tunacliffe Meadow, the cliff being the formerly fairly steep drop down to the Mersey valley which is still apparent in places. This name is interesting because it refers to habitation (A.S. *tun* – village, farm, etc.; *clif* – cliff), the cliff near the village or farm. The two Tunacliffe fields are to the north of Fairy Lane; on the 1876 Ordnancy Survey map to the south of Fairy Lane is shown a group of mounds, but they may be no more than glacial deposit.

So far as Ashton is concerned, the place-name itself is really sufficient evidence for late Anglo-Saxon settlement (village, farm near the ash trees). It would, like Sale, be a pre-Conquest township; among the field-names is a moot field. The moot field

Plate 1: Indications of medieval arable strip-farming are seen here. The ridge and furrow is quite apparent when on the site, but requires the shadow cast by the trees for the camera to pick it up. The distance between the centres of the ridges is 30 ft. (9 metres). The strips were named in the Enclosure Schedule as furlongs and doles; this, coupled with the fact that each strip was individually owned, is certain evidence of their early origin. The strip nearest to the conjectural area of early habitation is named as Nearer Furlong.

was the meeting place for the community to settle minor disputes and frame local laws; needless to say, this state of affairs was abolished after the Conquest.

Other field-names in Ashton of Anglo-Saxon origin include Stagoe Bottoms and Head (A.S. *staegel* – steep) and Stocky Field (A.S. *stocc lif* – habitation).

The 1806 Enclosure map and schedule provide plenty of evidence for medieval farming in Sale but, before dealing with it, it may be best to take a brief look at farming in north-east Cheshire generally during the Middle Ages. The popular view of medieval farming in England (and, indeed, the correct view for most of the country) is of the manor being divided into three great open fields, which had developed from the older, two-field system; the three fields rotating between spring corn, winter corn and fallow, with a shortage of pasture and meadow land inhibiting cattle farming.

Such was not the case generally in Cheshire. Open-field farming tended to be based on a two-field or even a multi-field system, with arable farming just sufficient for subsistence and the emphasis on pasture farming, due to the land not being the most suitable for growing corn, and the presence of an abundance of pasture. This is a general picture of Cheshire and, of course, there were exceptions, Wirral being one of them. South and west Cheshire specialised in dairy cattle while our own area, north

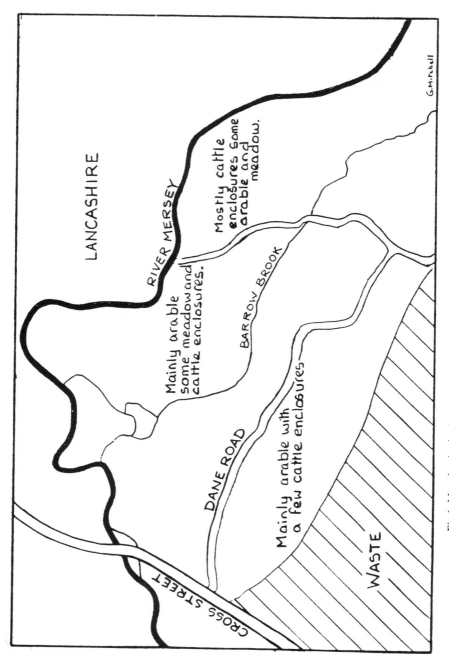

Fig.1: Map showing land-use in Sale during the Middle Ages based on field-names.

Cheshire, concentrated on cattle rearing and fattening due to the abundance of grass for pasture for summer feeding, and for hay production for winter feeding.

The medieval field-names that can be identified in the 1806 Enclosure schedule roughly bear out this picture of farming in our part of Cheshire during the Middle Ages. So far as arable farming is concerned the field-names include loonts – loonts or loons were arable strips; buts – the headland where the plough turned after completing a furrow length (furlong) and shots which meant the same thing.

There were also doles which, in Wirral, meant meadow land but in Macclesfield, according to Joan Beck, were arable; this was also the case in Sale. The 1806 map shows doles which are divided into strips typical of open field arable farming and, furthermore, at that late date the strips were still not enclosed and each one belonged to a different principal landowner.

The overall picture of medieval farming in Sale is one of a balance between cattle production and arable farming. To show this in a little more detail, it will be best to divide Sale into four areas. Area 1, bounded by Cross Street, the Mersey, Dane Road and a continuation of Old Hall Road to the Mersey; Area 2, bounded by the Mersey, Wythenshawe Road and Fairy Lane, the Northenden boundary and Old Hall Road; Area 3, bounded by Cross Street, School Road, the moor or waste, Dane Road and part of Temple Road; Area 4, bounded by School Road and Broad Road, Wythenshawe Road and part of Northenden Road in the north, the Northenden boundary in the east, Baguley Brook in the south and Washway Road in the west; this latter area was the waste or common in the Middle Ages and constituted nearly two-thirds of Sale.

Area 1 tended to be mainly arable with some meadow and a few heys (enclosures for cattle).

Area 2 had a preponderance of heys with some arable and a small amount of meadow.

Area 3 was mainly arable with one or two cattle heys.

Area 4 was the waste (Sale Moor) but some of the southern part was used for cattle heys, in what is now the Gawsworth Road – Alderley Road area. By the 17th century the south-west part of the moor that is, the area lying roughly south of Marsland Road as far as Baguley Brook, was cultivated in the form of fields anything from one to twelve acres in extent, enclosed by hedges. The 1806 map shows that the hedgerows were planted before the Bridgewater Canal was dug in the 18th century. These enclosures are distinct from the 1805 Act of Enclosure and were the result of agreement between the landowners.

Until the 17th century enclosures, Sale Moor had extended along the entire length of Washway Road from the Timperley boundary to School Road. The cattle heys on the moor were close to a now lost road on the Northenden boundary and, therefore, the cattle could be driven along this road to the pasture near the Mersey and eventually, it is to be supposed, to the markets at Altrincham and Stockport.

The crops grown in north Cheshire during the Middle Ages were mainly peas and beans, barley for bread and beer, and hay for the use of cattle through the winter. On a national level the amount of meadow available for hay production was limited and highly prized, more so than good arable land; but in Sale and Ashton and other places along the Mersey valley there was a plentiful supply of lush water meadows or "ees" to use the Anglo-Saxon term. Fish would provide an additional source of food.

The beef reared in Sale and the rest of north Cheshire would not be consumed by the ordinary serf. An indication of this is to be found in the English language after the Conquest; while the names of living animals ox, cow, steer, sheep, swine, deer, fowl are Anglo-Saxon, which remained the language of the common people, the terms applied to the flesh beef, mutton, pork, venison, pullet are Norman-French, with an exception being bacon, the only animal flesh which the common people used, apart from the entrails, etc. which were known as umbles – hence the term umble pie as it should be pronounced. Before ending this chapter, reference should be made again to the 12th century grant of land mentioned earlier.

The deed was translated from the medieval Latin by the late Hilda Lofthouse, formerly Chethams' librarian and it reads as follows:

'Let it appear &c. that I Thomas son of Richard de Hyde have given &c. to Henry de Trafford and his heirs all my land in the township of Sale within these boundaries;
beginning at the Oldhey and continuing between barfotehalt and merce going down to the water of Merce To have and to hold of me &c. paying to me and to my heirs an annual rent of one iron barbed arrow on the feast of St. Martin in the winter for all services, customs and claims.
Witnesses
Dominus Godfrey de Chedle, William de Bagguley, William de Carington, Thomas de Ashton, Richard de Moston and others.'

I think it safe to deduce from the foregoing that the northern boundary of the pre-Conquest township of Sale lay about one-third of a mile north of the present course of the Mersey, and at this point it should be explained that the term township and, later, the manor includes all the land within the boundaries, the arable and pasture as well as the woodland and waste and any fisheries there may be.

The piece of land referred to in the deed can be easily identified as the locations have existed until modern times; the name "barfotehalt" being preserved in Barfoot Bridge, the 18th century aqueduct carrying the canal over the Mersey at Stretford, and the Oldhey is shown on a Trafford Estate map of 1782. Barfote (A.S. *baerfot* – barefoot) is self-explanatory, while halt is a corruption of *halh* – the confluence of two rivers. The 1782 map shows what has formerly been the confluence of two channels of the Mersey just to the east of Barfoot Bridge with Old Hey against the west bank of the canal.

The northernmost of the two river channels can still be seen; the main road (A56) is carried over it by Eye Platt New Bridge and the southern channel is still, roughly, the present course of the Mersey, altered slightly some years ago when the eastern length of the M63 motorway was constructed.

We can conclude, therefore, by saying that some time before the Conquest the river Mersey in our area flowed along a channel which is crossed by Eye Platt New Bridge, and that is where the northern boundary of Sale and, consequently, Cheshire was. The grant of land to Henry de Trafford was, possibly, preparatory to settling the Lancashire boundary, Lancashire being first mentioned as a separate county in 1182 — about the date the deed was drawn up.

Further to the east of the A56, between there and Jackson's Boat, there are places where the Lancashire boundary is on the Cheshire side of the river; this is probably due to minor changes in the course of the river since the time the county boundaries were finally fixed.

Sources for Chapter 1 – The Beginnings of Sale

Ordnance Survey map, 1876.

Transactions Lancashire and Cheshire Antiquarian Society, vol. 19, 1901.

Whitaker, J. History of Manchester, vol. 1, 1771.

Lancashire MSS, vol. 25, p.180.

Sale Moor Enclosure Award, 1807.

Cornwall – Legh Muniments.

Plate 1a: Although Sale Old Hall dovecote shown here about 1965 is, like the Hall, a Gothic Revival structure, there is more than half a century between the two. The date 1895 was once given to me for the dovecote which is probably correct, as it is not shown on any map before the 25 inch Ordnance Survey of 1897.

The medieval manor house of the Masseys probably had a dovecote as, by law, only the lord of the manor could have one and so to possess one was a mark of one's station in life. Documentary evidence shows that the Hall had a dovecote in the 18th century which may have been demolished when the property was bought by Mary Worthington.

Photo R. Petrie

2

Land Tenure

The feudal system proper, evolved on the Continent and was a result of the Roman Empire being overrun by the barbaric tribes who, having occupied the territory, were confronted with the task of defending it and cultivating the land. Consequently, in the absence of a standing army and being economically incapable of maintaining one, they resorted to the plan of the leader's letting out the greater portion of the lands to his followers, on condition of their rendering military service when required to do so.

The system of feudalism, therefore, was as much dictated by military needs as social and economic ones. By the time of the Norman Conquest of England, the feudal system was fully established on the Continent and was introduced to England by William, with one important difference.

On the Continent the monarch let out most of his land to tenants-in-chief, who swore service to the monarch. Then the tenants-in-chief let most of this land to sub-tenants who swore service to them but not to the monarch; this could go on through several stages. In England, however, after the Conquest William exacted the oath from all sub-tenants and, to strengthen his position still further, distributed the fees (or grants of land) of his tenants-in-chief in different parts of the country. For example, the Earl of Moreton had land as far apart as Cornwall, Northampton, York and Sussex, thus making it difficult to mount a revolt against the King.

This was the system which operated in Normandy in contrast to the rest of the Continent; the Normans not being French, but of the same Gothic origin as the English. They were by origin Norse, hence the name Norman, or North man. The Normans, although they abandoned their own Nordic language, adopted a form of French which brought that language to its highest level, from what the Normans regarded as a barbaric jargon; this Norman–French, introduced by them to England, became the language of the ruling class.

Under William the Anglo-Saxon shires became counties; each administered by a tenant-in-chief called a count, although later the Anglo-Saxon title of earl re-asserted itself. The first Norman tenant-in-chief of the county of Chester (Cheshire) was Gherbod in 1070, but he resigned the following year and William appointed his nephew Hugh Lupus (Hugh the Wolf) who, apart from the Bishop of Chester, was the only tenant-in-chief in the county.

Among Hugh's tenants, or barons, was William FitzNigel who, as hereditary Constable of Chester, was Hugh's chief baron; he held thirty manors, his seat or barony being Halton, among the manors he held was that of Sale. We use the term "held" at this period because, in theory, the king owned all land, his tenants-in-chief merely holding it on his behalf, and it was not until after the Reformation that land became a commodity which could be bought and sold. In practice, of course, the tenants were to all intents and purposes landowners and, on a tenant's death, his heir inherited the land as well as personal possessions.

Norman lords of the manor were known as Geoffrey de Warburton, Adam de Carrington, etc. (Geoffrey of Warburton, Adam of Carrington) from the names of the Anglo-Saxon townships which they expropriated; therefore, paradoxically, anyone today with an Anglo-Saxon place-name for their surname can in theory, but rarely in practice, trace their ancestry back to a Norman lord of the manor; surnames generally, beginning to appear during the 12th century.

Half of the manor of Sale was held by Thomas de Sale from William FitzNigel, date unknown, but probably in the second half of the 12th century. The other half of Sale was held from William FitzNigel who was Constable of Chester and Baron of Halton, by Adam de Carrington, then by Adam de Dutton from Carrington and finally by Richard Massey (sometimes described as Richard le Massey de Sale) in 1187; Richard Massey was a member of a younger branch of the Masseys, Barons of Dunham. In 1189 Richard Massey became possessed of half of the manors of Godley and Newton.

Thomas de Sale apparently had no male heir as his half of the manor of Sale passed to John Holt who married Sale's daughter, Ellen. By the 17th century both the Holts and the Masseys had sold land to various people including, in the case of John Holt's descendant Thomas, to Sir George Booth of Dunham Massey in 1604, the Booths later becoming the Earls of Stamford.

The Masseys retained most of their half of Sale, and an indenture of circa 1403 shows that they had acquired one quarter of another manor at Mattley and, by the early part of the 16th century, Hamon Massey also held land in Walton from the Warburtons, land in Hale, Mottram (in Longdendale) and Hollingworth and in Stockport, Northenden and Ringway.

Hamon Massey (also known as Hamlette) could not be accused of living a sheltered life; he died about 1556, his will stating his wish to be buried in the chancel of Ashton Church, discloses that he had four illegitimate sons and an illegitimate daughter. His son and heir, Richard, was aged 12.

Richard Massey died on January 16, 1603 and an inquisition post mortem of his estate was taken at Sandbach the following October 14. From this we learn that Richard's demesne, that is the part of the estate which is usually retained for the lord of the manor and his family, was held by 15 tenants and consisted of 100 acres of (arable) land, 40 acres of meadow, 100 acres of pasture, 10 acres of woodland and 40 acres of moor and moss in Sale, Walton, Northenden and Ringway. This land was let at will for a term of ten years.

He was also in possession of half the manor of Sale and 200 acres of land, 40 acres of meadow, 200 acres of pasture, 100 acres of woodland, 500 acres of moor and moss and one fish pond in Sale, Walton and Northenden, in addition to half the manor of Godley which included a water mill, 80 acres of land, 20 acres of meadow, 200 acres of pasture, 100 acres of woodland, 200 acres of moor and 100 acres of gorse and heath; also a quarter of the manor of Mattley and one-sixth of the manor of Newton, with 100 acres of land, 20 acres of meadow, 100 acres of pasture, 20 acres of woodland, 100 acres of moor, also 100 acres of gorse and heath in Mattley, Newton and Mottram-in-Longdendale.

Richard Massey also possessed 40 acres of land, 10 acres of meadow, 40 acres of pasture and 3 acres of woodland in Hale. His half of the manor of Sale was held from Peter Warburton of Arley (a descendant of Adam de Dutton) in socage, that is, for services excluding military service which did not signify anything by this period. Finally, he also held the manor of Tintwistle by a twentieth part of a knight's fee (£10 a year). The lands in Ringway and Hale were held from Sir Edward Staveley.

Plate 2: The 19th century datestone from Sale Old Hall. Frost damage has probably caused the date 1840 to break away.

The acreage listed above would be in Cheshire acres which should be multiplied by 2.1 to convert to statute acres; the origin of the Cheshire acre will be dealt with briefly in a later chapter.

This will be a suitable point at which to make some mention of Sale Old Hall. The Hall stood, within living memory, to the south side of Rifle Road and was rebuilt in 1840 by Mrs. Mary Worthington who had bought the existing building. The Hall was over two centuries old at the time and its condition may have been such, that Mrs. Worthington had no other option than to demolish and rebuild.

The 1840 building was in turn demolished in 1920, and the datestone was removed and fixed to the lodge inside the entrance to Worthington (then Sale) Park; it has an inscription in relief, JM 1600 and below formerly, MW 1840. The inscription stands for James Massey and the supposed date of the erection of the earlier building but, as we have seen from the inquisition post mortem above, Richard Massey lived until 1603 his heir James who, after all, was only ten years old not succeeding until that year.

However, the Hall was probably erected somewhere near that date; an estate map of Sale of 1801 shows Sale Old Hall in plan; the building having two wings and a central porch in the typical "E" plan of the Elizabethan and Jacobean period. It was a brick Hall as indicated by a large quantity of 2½in. (65mm) thick bricks found by digging on the site before it was lost to the construction of the motorway.

The Elizabethan or Jacobean building will, in turn, have replaced a medieval timber-frame manor house which may not have been on the same site. The medieval hall of the neighbouring manor of Baguley still survives, and is in process of restoration; we are fortunate enough to have on our doorstep one of the most important medieval timber-frame buildings in the country in Baguley Hall which is, according to the architectural historians, a survival of pre-Conquest building traditions which survived into the 14th century, when Baguley Hall was built.

James Massey who, as stated, inherited the estates at Sale and other places in 1603 at the age of ten, died in 1649 leaving two sons Richard and William. Richard, the heir, settled Sale Old Hall and the demesne lands in 1684 on his eldest daughter, Katherine, who married Robert Malyn. Meanwhile William, James's younger son, married Ursula Domville which brought him the Hall estate in Lymm and an estate in Audlem. He built a house in 1688 in Fairy Lane known as Sale New Hall which was demolished in 1953.

Robert and Katherine Malyn's son, Massey Malyn, was Rector of the Parish from 1717 until his death in 1729; his sisters and co-heirs Katherine and Ann married, respectively, Walter Noble and Peter Mainwaring M.D. The Egertons of Tatton bought the Noble estate, Dr. Mainwaring bequeathing his estate to the Leghs of East Hall, High Legh. And so the male line of the Masseys of Sale died out before the end of the 17th century, having held their estate here for 500 years; in the following century, through inheritance and purchase, the principal landowners were the Earl of

Plate 3: The photograph above shows some ornamental stone parapet from the garden walls of the Hall, now used as a garden boundary wall at a house in Skaife Road.

Stamford and Warrington, the Leghs and Egertons and, later, Charles White, all of whom will be met with again when we deal with the Enclosure Act of 1805.

The land tenure in Ashton is rather obscure. It appears that in the 14th century half of the manor was held by the Boydells of Dodleston and the other half held by the family of Asheton, probably from the barons of Dunham Massey. Eventually most of Ashton was possessed by the Breretons of Handforth who sold the estate to Sir Joshua Allen (later Viscount Allen of Stillorgan, Ireland).

In 1749, the Allens sold Ashton to the Earl of Warrington, and it descended to the Earl of Stamford; Samuel Brooks, the Manchester banker, bought all the Stamford land in Ashton in 1852.

Even the ecclesiastical boundaries of Ashton are obscure. The Parish of Ashton-on-Mersey until the second half of the 19th century included the whole of the township of Sale, but only part of Ashton township, the rest of Ashton belonging to the Parish of Bowdon. Incredibly, the boundaries of these two parts were not fully known. Sale was the major part of the Parish and of the three churchwardens, one was chosen by the Rector, another by the occupant of Sale Old Hall and the third by the township of Sale. It was not until 1921 that a people's warden was appointed for Ashton; Sale Old Hall having been demolished the previous year.

The manor of Sale did not have its own corn-mill, the mill being at Ashton. I. J. E. Renshaw in his history of Ashton suggested that this was a windmill; however, the Ashton Tithe Map shows a field called Mill Ground, situated against the river bank, roughly to the north of St. Martin's Church and it is likely that this is the site of a former water-mill.

In 1525 James Massey had a dispute with Hugh Tipping, the Rector, over the tithe of the corn-mill. The dispute went to arbitration, the result being that James and his heirs had to pay to Hugh and his assigns an annual payment for the tithe of the mill.

The 17th century enclosures by agreement, mentioned in the previous chapter, brought more land into cultivation from the moor; the earliest record we have of this being in 1621; this increased the number of small tenanted farms in the 18th and 19th centuries. Some of these existed well into the 20th century and are still remembered; an example being Lime Tree Farm, Baguley Lane, the site of which is now occupied by the school; this farm was owned by George John Legh and William Egerton in 1806 and was let to a tenant; part of the land, now occupied by Cranston Drive and Dunollie Road was called Moor Field, indicating its origin.

Sale Moor, the subject of the 1805 Enclosure Act was, in the second half of the nineteenth century, virtually entirely used for the building of substantial detached and semi-detached houses, while the area enclosed in the 17th century remained agricultural until the building boom of the 1920s and, more especially, the 1930s.

Sources for Chapter 2 – Land Tenure

Lancashire MSS, vol. 16.

Notitia Cestriensis.

Journal of Society of Antiquaries, vol. 60.

Sale Moor Enclosure Award, 1806–7.

Cornwall–Legh Muniments.

3

The Road System

"The rolling English drunkard made the rolling English road" wrote G. K. Chesterton; this is not only an affront to drunkards, particularly the English variety, but is patently untrue. Most of our roads, until a century or so ago, were medieval in origin. The Roman roads ran straight as far as possible, deviating only to avoid sometimes a hill, or to approach a fordable part of a river; for they were purpose-built military roads and had only natural features to obstruct their course. Interestingly, they were constructed almost exactly the same as roads built in modern times by sappers of the Royal Engineers.

The medieval roads, on the other hand, came into being to serve the needs of agriculture. The farming of the land took priority and the road was merely the means of serving it, no matter whether its purpose was to get from one village to another or merely a way between fields; and so wherever the land rose or fell making ploughing difficult, or where the plough stopped short of a watercourse, that is where the road was often established.

When the first settlement was founded in Sale, what is now Cross Street and Washway Road was already in existence as part of the Roman road from Chester to Manchester. Incidentally, any English place-name containing the element chester, cester or similar (A.S. *ceaster*) is almost invariably a former Roman site. It is likely that the next oldest road, of pre-Conquest origin, followed the line of Dane Road, part of Old Hall Road, Wythenshawe Road and Fairy Lane, possibly to an early settlement in that area. The earliest cultivated land in Sale was in the Mersey valley and so other roads had to give access to the valley, Cow Lane being one such example. Cow Lane, from Arnesby Avenue, is a gentle slope down from the steep edge of the valley, a field-name at this point being Cliff Brow.

Another road of some importance formerly existed on which, in 1973, I carried out some coarse archaeology; this is a term which I use to describe the digging and scraping carried out by people like myself with little or no training in the subject. Such activities should be confined to sites of no interest to the professional archaeologist. The road in question originally crossed the Mersey by means of a ford in the vicinity

Plate 4: The bridge over Baguley Brook at the Wythenshawe boundary which probably dates from the 18th century and carried a road over the brook which, at that period, formed part of a road from Altrincham, through Chorlton, to Manchester.

of Barlow Hall in Chorlton and ran along Sale's eastern boundary with Northenden (Wythenshawe being part of Northenden township) to at least as far as Baguley where it crossed the brook.

The possibility that a road may have existed at this point first occurred to me after seeing a well-built stone bridge of possibly 18th century date which spans Baguley Brook at the Sale–Northenden boundary. This bridge although measuring almost 10ft. (3 metres) between the ramparts, serves at present only to carry a narrow footpath over the brook to Woodiwiss Lane; it therefore seemed reasonable to assume that the footpath had been at one time a road of a reasonable width for its period assuming that it was, say, 18th century.

A section cut out about 30 metres north of the bridge revealed a pebble road surface nearly 8ft. (2.5 metres) in width about 3ins. (80mm) below the surface. At this stage I consulted a map of Wythenshawe of 1641 which showed Baguley Brook fordable at the point where the road now is.

A field-name in the area where the dig had been made was Road Hey, the 'hey' element indicating that the road is older than the bridge. The field-name Gate Field near to the Mersey and adjoining the theoretical line of the road suggested that the road had run all the way along Sale's eastern boundary to the river; the name 'gate' is Middle English and means a road which is a right of way.

More probing and digging uncovered further sections of the road in two places; one near the University playing fields and the other near the golf course, close to the river, and about 6ins. (150mm) below the surface.

The road is almost certainly medieval in origin and provided an alternative to the main road as a means of crossing the Mersey. The ford at Crossford was probably no longer usable by the Middle Ages, as it is referred to in 1367 as Cross Ferry and a field near the present Crossford Bridge was called Boat Hey.

The northern part of the lost road possibly fell into disuse as a highway in the later Middle Ages as by 1538 there was a bridge at Crossford. Part of the southern

Plate 5: The overgrown watercourse running across the photograph divides the former townships of Sale and Northenden. From the late 11th century it was also the boundary between the Hundreds of Bucklow and Macclesfield. The land which can be seen on the far side of the watercourse is part of Sale and was formerly called Gate Field.

The line of trees is part of a former hedge which continues along Fairy Lane. For those who subscribe to the Hooper method of hedge-dating it appears to be several centuries old and possibly at one time divided the arable and meadow from the pasture.

part of the road continued to be used by local people at least; in a case heard at Knutsford assizes in 1779 reference was made to "part of an ancient highway between Chorton with Hardy and the . . . parish of Ashton" (Sale being part of Ashton parish) and went on to say that "formerly the highway from Altringham to Manchester was over Sale Moor and thro the ford in Chorton".

This was followed by the statement that Dane Road "meets the ancient highway at a place called the Green in Sale and that . . . it . . . leads from the Green towards Chorton". So the route of the road which would be used to avoid paying tolls on the main road, which was turnpiked by this time, was from Altrincham Road and Wythenshawe Road in Baguley, Woodiwiss Lane, over the stone bridge spanning Baguley Brook, and following Sale's eastern boundary for some distance. Then along Gratrix Lane, crossing Northenden Road to follow Wythenshawe Road, Old Hall Road (the Green) and then over Jackson's Ford which was some distance downstream from Jackson's Boat.

The full length of the meandering road in its original course from Baguley Brook to the Mersey was about 1¾ miles; it followed a watercourse which flowed from the brook to the river, passing under Northenden Road near Boundary Grove and forming the boundary between Sale and Northenden and the Hundreds of Bucklow and Macclesfield, Sale being in the Bucklow Hundred; perhaps a brief reference to the origin of the Hundreds would not be out of place at this point.

During the tenth century the Anglo-Saxon shires were, for administrative purposes, divided into a number of Hundreds, each of which was calculated as being of sufficient size to maintain a hundred families, each Hundred taking its name from the place where a court was held every four weeks. The Hundreds survived the Norman Conquest and in 1086 there were ten in Cheshire, later reduced to eight; at this time Northenden was taken out of the Bucklow Hundred and became part of the Macclesfield Hundred. The Hundreds then remained unchanged until 1894 when they were superseded by the Rural Districts.

The bridge which carried the lost road over Baguley Brook is wide enough to take carts and was probably used by pack-horses, as the ramparts are excessively low and would not obstruct the low-slung packs. The pack-horse or pack-mule was the most common method of transporting goods up to the canal age; there is evidence that mule-breeding was practised at Sale New Hall in the 18th century.

To return to the main road, we know that a bridge carried Cross Street over the Mersey in 1538 from a statement by Henry VIII's antiquary, John Leland that year. "I rode over Mersey Water by a great bridge of tymbre caullid Crosford Bridge" wrote Leland. To describe the bridge as "great" would not refer to the height; Crossford Bridge did not need to be high as the Mersey was not navigable so far upstream; Leland must have meant the length of the bridge.

The river at that spot will have been quite wide, especially in times of flood, but fairly shallow in normal times, which is why it was once fordable there. This is supported by later evidence when, in 1753, the Commissioners of the Longford Turnpike advertised for persons "willing to undertake to raise the Road from Crossford Bridge . . . so high as to be secure from the Floods, with Ramparts and Arches in proper Places . . .".

There may have been a period in the 16th century some time after Leland's itinerary when there was no bridge at Crossford at all. Saxton's map of Cheshire of 1577 does not show a bridge there and Hollingworth writing in 1656 says "Anno 1577. Crosford or Crosferry Bridge was begunne to be taken care of that it might be reedifyed [rebuilt] and built of stone . . . the bridge was builded in the manner that now it is. The yeare following".

It was probably this bridge which was broken down on Government orders to delay the Jacobites' advance in 1745.

The Statute of Bridges of 1530 made the inhabitants of a county responsible for the repair of bridges and Crossford Bridge was maintained by Lancashire. The county was also responsible for maintaining the road for 100 yards (92 metres) at each end of the bridge. Two ancient stones still exist at the edge of the footpath on Cross Street and the inscription can still be faintly made out. One of them, near the Crossfords public house reads County Palatine of Lancaster and the other, near the Royal Garage, reads County Palatine of Chester, marking the limit of the distance from the bridge that Lancashire was responsible for keeping in repair.

If a private person built a bridge, then he was responsible for its upkeep and was permitted to take tolls from users of the bridge. There were sometimes attempts by neighbouring landowners to exact tolls at public bridges. In 1621 at the Lancashire Quarter Sessions it was stated "The Justices here present are of opinion that if any toll or stellage be taken for the carriage over Crossford Bridge . . . the same is extortion and ought not to be taken or paid".

The bridgemaster's report of 1782 describes Crossford Bridge as "a very firm good bridge" and that it had one arch with a span of 66ft. (20 metres), the width of the roadway on the bridge being 18ft. 4ins. (5.5 metres).

In 1907 Crossford Bridge was widened and in 1961 the height of the parapets was increased when the steel bridge was erected to carry the south-west bound traffic.

The names Crossford and Cross Street are supposedly derived from the existence of a cross which, it is said, stood at the north end of the bridge in pre-Reformation times. The Great Stone at Stretford is the base of a cross and it has been suggested that it originally stood at Crossford Bridge.

There are references in the 18th century to the terrible condition of Cross Street, which is not surprising as all the evidence nationally tends to show that the highways were in far better condition during the Middle Ages, when the duty to repair the highways was enforced by the manorial court. The manorial system having come to an end, an Act was passed in 1555 which made the parish responsible for the repairs and provided for the annual election by the vestry of two Surveyors of Highways.

The vestry was the body of ley, or rate payers which met regularly in the parish or township to administer local affairs.

The Surveyors' job was to see that the landowners supplied carts and horses and that every able-bodied labourer attended for four and, later, six consecutive days in the year for work on roads. This forced labour was known as Statute Labour and it did little to improve the condition of the roads which continued to deteriorate. In an effort to improve the main roads turnpike trusts were set up under local Acts.

On December 5, 1764 a meeting of "Gentlemen in the Counties of Chester and Lancaster" was called at the Unicorn in Altrincham, to consider an application to turnpike the section of the main road from Crossford Bridge to Altrincham; the length from Crossford Bridge to Manchester had been turnpiked in 1750.

The Washway Turnpike Act as it was called was passed in 1765 and £500 was borrowed on the credit of the tolls in order to build a toll house, erect bars and to widen and repair the road. The toll house at Crossford Bridge occupied about half the width of the road and was situated just inside the Ashton boundary next to the Bridge Inn, Stretford, which, after four changes of name since 1975 is, at the time of writing, called Crossfords. The repair of the road was financed by the tolls and augmented with Statute Labour.

A description of the main road just prior to its being turnpiked states that it was "exceedingly deep, ruinous, and dangerous . . .". In 1771, six years after it had been turnpiked, Arthur Young the agricultural theorist travelled along it and writes of it as "a paved causeway, done in so wretched a manner that it is cut into continuous holes. For it is so narrow that only one carriage can move at a time and that, consequently, in a line of ruts . . .".

Some idea of the standard of repair may be gleaned from an entry in the Sale township minutes of July 30, 1810 which orders that "the Commissioners of the Washway Turnpike road shall pay to the Surveyors . . . the Sum of £5 for Sods taken for the use of the said Turnpike Road . . ." This unsatisfactory state of affairs continued until well into the second half of the 19th century; in 1878 an Act was passed providing that all roads disturnpiked after 1871 should become main roads and local authorities could claim reimbursement of half the cost of repairing them from the Quarter Sessions.

The Crossford toll-bar was abolished in 1885 and three years later the Local Government Act put the burden of main roads on the new county councils.

When the canal was constructed in the 18th century, it is likely that the course of Broad Road was changed, as the sharp turn at Priory Road in order to meet the canal bridge looks artificial, unlike a naturally winding road. It is to be supposed that Broad Lane, as it was formerly called, continued to Cross Street before the 1760s; the 1806 township map shows a narrow field (no. 88 on the map) adjoining Cross Street near Dargle Road. This field may have been the western end of Broad Lane; a field bordering it is called Lane Field.

Before the enclosure of Sale Moor, Marsland Road between the canal bridge and Washway Road ran in a more northerly direction than at present and joined Washway Road opposite Barkers Lane, being altered to its present form by the Enclosure Commissioners in 1805–7. The Commissioners laid out a number of roads across Sale Moor and these will be mentioned in a later chapter.

Prior to the 1860s all the roads in Sale with the exception of the main road were called lanes. In 1867, Northenden Road between the Legh Arms and Sale station, which was originally known as Sale Moor station, was called Moor Lane; another part, from the Legh Arms to Gratrix Lane, was called Northenden Road, and the final length between Gratrix Lane and the Northenden boundary was still known by its old name of Hart Lane. The following year it was all called Northenden Road. Wardle Road, for another example was called Wardle Lane until 1866.

The Sale township minutes from 1805 make frequent references to the repair of the roads; that year it was ordered that "the Causeways in Dean Lane [Dane Road] be repaired", the causeway would be used by pack-horses. In 1836 it was ordered that guide posts were to be erected "at the end of the Highway near the Volunteer . . . and at the end of the Highway leading from Marsland's Bridge to the Washway Turnpike Road", they were to be inscribed "To Northen 2 Miles". At this point it may be said that washway roads in the 18th and 19th centuries were roads constructed in an attempt to make rainwater assist in the repair of them, by the road being in a concave form rather than having a camber, with the intention that the water would wash the road clean and be conducted away through a side outlet.

Increased traffic in the 18th century brought a corresponding increase in the number of inns in places where they were likely to attract custom. Cross Street was obviously a suitable place and the Bull's Head, Volunteer and Waggon and Horses appeared; the first two were rebuilt in Victoria's reign and the Waggon and Horses was considerably altered.

The present Lindow Tavern on Northenden Road, at the corner of Gratrix Lane, is on the site of an earlier public house, described in the 1806 Enclosure schedule as "Lindow building and garden". It was owned by Edward Gratrix and occupied by Peter Gratrix who, like other innkeepers of the time, was also a farmer being the tenant of more than 30 acres. The Lindow was in a suitable position, being on the road to Northenden and Stockport and, as mentioned previously, Gratrix Lane was part of a highway from Altrincham to Manchester.

Apart from the main road, the first time that roads in Sale were planned was in the 1805–7 Enclosure period. A second stage of planned road construction was carried out by Samuel Brooks about the middle of the 19th century. The two most notable examples are Brooklands Road and the Avenue, or Brooks Avenue as it was formerly called; both of these roads were laid out as excellent examples of landscaped urban roads thrusting into the then still rural scene.

It may be said at this point that the name Brooklands arose by virtue of Brooks selling land to the railway company on the understanding that the station was named Brooklands; this gave rise to the area around the station becoming known as Brooklands although, strictly speaking, people in that area live either in Sale or Baguley, depending on which side of Baguley Brook they are.

The house-building era which began in Sale and Ashton in the second half of the 19th century and, interrupted by two wars, continued to the 1960s, produced the large network of roads which now covers the area.

Sources for Chapter 3 – The Road System

Richard Martinscroft's map of Wythenshawe, 1641.

Sale Enclosure map, 1806.

Cornwall–Legh Muniments.

John Leland's Itinerary, 1538.

Manchester Mercury, December 11, 1753; May 28, 1765.

An Account and Admeasurement of the Public Bridges within the Hundred of Salford. By Edmond Holme, Bridge-master. 1782. p. 74.

Cheshire Notes and Queries, vol. 5, p. 69.

Transactions Lancashire and Cheshire Antiquarian Society, vol. 5, 1888.

Sale Township Minutes.

Map of estates in Sale of G. J. Legh, 1801.

Sale Rate Books.

Hollingworth, R. An History of the Towne of Manchester, c.1656, pub. 1839.

Ormerod, G. History of the County Palatine of Chester, 2nd ed. 1882.

Johnson's map of Parish of Manchester, c.1820.

House of Commons Journals, February 12, 1765.

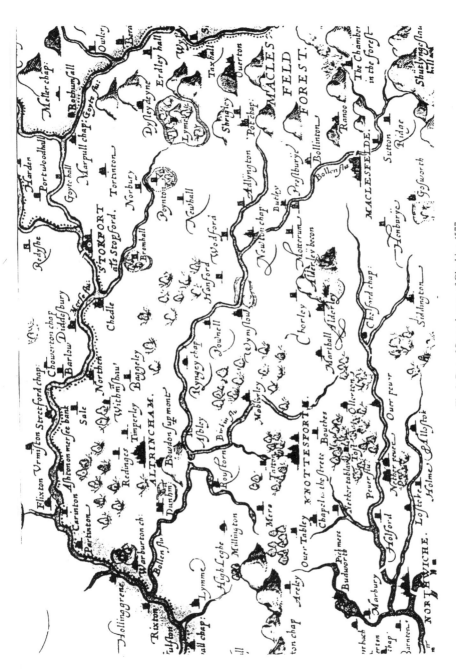

Fig 2: Part of Saxton's map of Cheshire, 1577

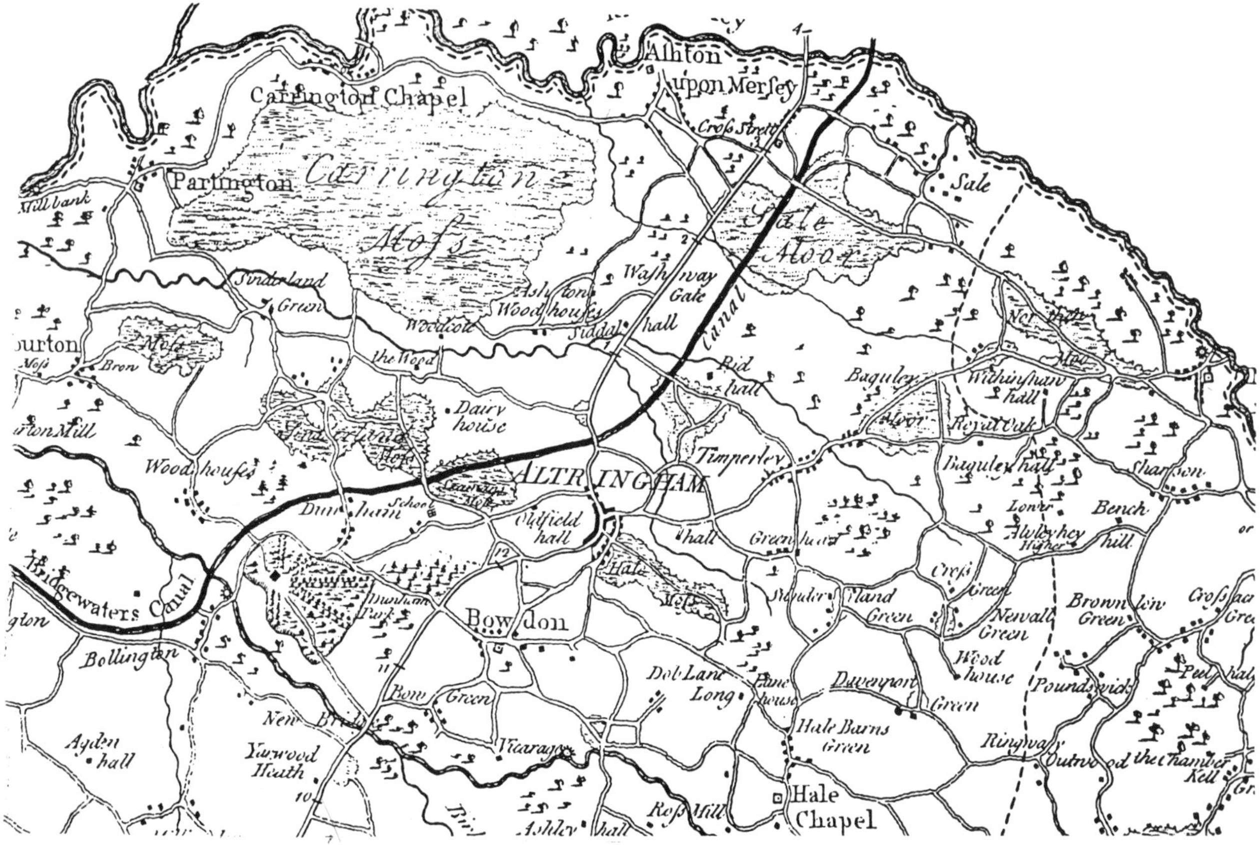

Fig 3: Part of Burdett's map of Cheshire, 1777.

4

Sale before the
Enclosure Act

After the feudal system had ended, conditions in this area changed very slowly; in north Cheshire peat continued to be used for fuel until the second half of the 18th century, when the canal was opened and coal brought from Worsley. The living conditions of the ordinary people were very poor and, until about 1540, they continued to live much as they had done from earlier times, with animals in their crude homes and an open fire in the room, the smoke escaping through a hole in the roof.

What kind of picture can be presented of Sale in the period between the end of the Middle Ages and the beginning of the 19th century? For the 19th century there are excellent local maps and, later, the Ordnance Survey; but from the 16th century to the 18th century, only maps of the whole county are available; the first map of Cheshire being that of Christopher Saxton 1577.

Saxton, of Dunningley, near Leeds, surveyed and drew maps of every county, the complete set being published in 1579. His map of Cheshire formed the basis of all succeeding maps of the county for practically 200 years. Harold Whitaker in his work on early Cheshire maps published in 1942, remarking on the symbols which Saxton used on his map, states that a church symbol stood for a village and a house represents a hamlet.

It seems more likely that the church symbol is meant to represent a church and nothing more; often, as in the case of Sale, a village is not in association with a church.

So far as the house symbol is concerned, Whitaker's opinion that it represents a hamlet can be ruled out, as a house is shown, for example, at Bramhall, Poynton and Lyme, and in these cases a park paling is shown enclosing the house, therefore any hamlet would have been demolished and rebuilt outside the paling when the park was constructed. The house symbol indicates the hall of the landed gentry, formerly the manor house. Sale is shown by a house symbol and Ashton by a church.

Saxton does not show Crossford Bridge, as mentioned in the previous chapter. Maps of Cheshire continued to be published throughout the 17th and 18th centuries, some of them on so small a scale as to verge on the ridiculous and most of them of

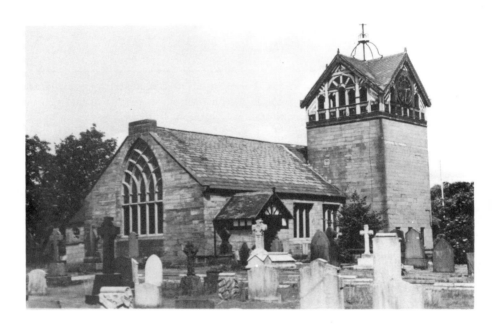

Plate 6: St. Martin's church, rebuilt in 1714 of sandstone in squared random rubble, is an example of a Gothic Survival church; that is, a church built quite out of period. It is late medieval in style with many features, including a double hammerbeam roof, normally found in a Perpendicular church of the 15th century.

As an example of Gothic Survival, St. Martin's is spoiled by a number of later additions, not the least being the tower erected in 1887. The porch has been altered, probably when the tower was built; a photograph taken before 1887 shows the porch to have had a semi-circular arch, not a feature of a Gothic building. The inner doorway, in contrast, is quite in accord with the style, having a Gothic arch, and it is possible that the porch is a later 18th or 19th century addition.

The tower and porch, however, are now part of the history of the building and the little church is well worth visiting.

little value to the historian. In 1777, however, a map of Cheshire appeared which can almost hold its own with the first Ordnance Survey map of Cheshire that appeared in its complete form 65 years later.

P. P. Burdett published, in 1777, the first map of Cheshire to be based on an exact survey by triangulation on the scale of one inch (25mm) to one mile. The map shows a wealth of detail including towns and villages; roads are accurately drawn and it is a valuable aid to the study of 18th century Cheshire.

On Saxton's 1577 map "Ashton on mersee bank" is shown by a church symbol and the medieval village was probably in close proximity to St. Martin's Church and Ashton Old Hall which was close by. Ashton would look the typical nucleated village settlement with church, hall and mill.

It has often been said that the medieval church of St. Martin was a timber-frame building, destroyed by a storm in 1703, and replaced by the present church in 1714. There is no evidence that the church was ever a timber building; on the contrary such evidence as there is suggests that it was built from stone and had an aisle. Burdett's 1777 map shows the church with a village straggling along the east side of Church Lane.

The house symbol representing Sale on Saxton's map is meant to be the former manor house of the Masseys, Sale Old Hall. There was certainly no priory at Sale, although a booklet was published in 1921 claiming the existence of one and even going into detail on the number of inmates. At the time of the Dissolution of the Monasteries there were only eleven religious houses in Cheshire and all of them are known. The booklet also states that Baguley Hall was a nunnery, pulled down the same time as the priory and a farmhouse built on the site; as mentioned earlier the existing building dates from the 14th century.

Some years ago I chanced on some evidence in the Cornwall–Legh muniments which puts the date of the building of the house known from the second half of the 19th century onwards as The Priory at about 1711. A dispute had occurred, involving Charles White who lived at The Priory, concerning the right of way on Dane Road in 1779 which went to litigation; in the course of giving evidence, a Joseph Bythell aged "76 and upwards" states that the house was built when he was about "8 or 9 years".

Even without this evidence there is no question of a priory ever having existed in Sale, as no land here was held by a religious order. A photograph exists which shows the cellars of the building, allegedly all that remained of the original "priory"; the cellars were constructed from brick and, although the oldest surviving brick dwelling in England, which is in Suffolk, dates from the late 13th century brick was not used as a building material in the north-west until after the Dissolution. The "priory" and the supposed Roman fort have given rise to published accounts of two buildings in Sale which never existed – few towns can match this.

The nearest industry to Sale in the 18th century was an ironworks at Partington; an advertisement in the Manchester Mercury in 1772 announced the auction of a rolling mill and paper mill in Partington "in the Center of an extensive Iron Manufactory"

Plate 7: Architectural historians divide domestic architecture into two main categories, "polite" and "vernacular". Polite architecture followed the fashion of the time and was generally confined to the homes of the wealthy; whereas vernacular architecture owes its varied styles to more local building traditions. Inevitably there are examples which fall somewhere between the two and Ashton New Hall may be said to illustrate this. On balance, the house is an example of polite architecture and is the earliest surviving example of its kind in Sale.

Although Ashton New Hall is built mainly of locally made bricks, the front elevation is constructed of a superior brick, all the brickwork being in Flemish bond. The house is late Georgian as indicated by the doorway with its style of pediment and fanlight, and the slender glazing bars in the windows.

Plate 8: This late 18th century example of vernacular architecture at the southern end of Wythenshawe Road is a type known as the double-pile Small House, the term meaning that the house is two rooms deep, giving a square plan, with a total of four rooms on each floor level. The house shown here is a typical example with a living room and parlour on the front and a kitchen and dairy at the back, with four bedrooms corresponding to the rooms below and a garret in the roof space.

In houses of this type all the rooms except the dairy have a fireplace on the side walls; also typical is the doorway placed off-centre to give a larger parlour and originally the door will have given entrance directly into the living room on the right. The staircase conforms to the standard plan, being placed between the kitchen and dairy; the brickwork at the front is in Flemish bond.

Houses like this one were built to accomodate the families of small tenant-farmers. In 1860 a shop was added and the house became a public-house called the Nag's Head and continued as such until 1912.

and a map of 1786 shows a slitting mill at Partington; these mills, situated on the Mersey bank, were water-driven. The rolling mill rolled the iron into lengths of bar and the slitting mill then cut the bar into lengths, usually for the manufacture of nails. Any industry in Sale would consist of handicrafts subordinate to the needs of agriculture.

Burdett's 1777 map shows a village on both sides of Cross Street between Chapel Road and Dane Road. This village was called Cross Street, one half lying in Ashton and the other half in Sale; the west carriageway of the A56 being the boundary between Ashton and Sale. The village of Sale is not shown nucleated but is rather scattered, consisting in the main of small farmhouses in the area of Fairy Lane, Old Hall Road and Dane Road east of Priory Road.

There was, however, a village green and pond, the site now occupied by the section of Old Hall Road between Wythenshawe Road and Dane Road, and by the end of the 18th century two rows of cottages had been erected opposite the green, the site being between nos. 100 and 120 Old Hall Road.

Sale village also had a pinfold situated at the junction of Temple Road and Dane Road on a site now occupied by an ornamental garden which forms an island in the road. The purpose of a pinfold or pound was to confine stray livestock until claimed by the owner.

In the 17th century this part of Sale (the village) was known as Lane End, the lane being Dane Road. There is an entry in Stretford parish register which reads as follows:

Mary Moores the dauter of John M.
of Sale commonly called lane end
being kild of wooster fight was
babtised the first day of feubruary
annoq domini 1651.

John Moores was evidently killed at the battle of Worcester at the end of the Civil War; he was probably on the side of Parliament, as the Royalists at Worcester were mainly Scots. James Massey of Sale Hall, on the other hand, was most likely a Royalist sympathiser as indicated by events when the war had finished. The Civil War ended in victory for Parliament; Cromwell's New Model Army was probably the most efficient in Europe and the modern Regular Army is directly descended from it. When the war had ended, there were reparations to be paid by those who had supported the Royalist cause, either actively or passively; to this end a schedule of the "delinquencies" of each Royalist was drawn up and the various ways in which he had offended were noted. The offender's estates were fairly valued and he was fined a sum in proportion to the value of his estate and the extent of his offence. In a list of the estates sequestrated in Cheshire is to be found "James Massey of Sale, Esqr. hath severall tenements in Mottram parish in lease, the rents whereof are sequestred . . .".

Plate 9: When more accommodation was needed than the double-pile Small House could provide, often when a small tenant-farmer increased the size of his holding, a sideways extension to the house was provided. Woodhouse Farm, Woodhouse Lane shown here is a typical example of this, conforming to the type in every respect.

It is a double-pile house with an extension to the left which has its own fireplace and chimney and formerly had an outside staircase serving a granary or storeroom. The dairy floor was originally 18 ins (450 mm.) below ground level to provide a cold floor; it has a vaulted ceiling of brick and the floor of the room above is flagged, the space between the flags and the brick arch beneath being packed with sand for additional insulation.

Some years ago the farmhouse, threatened with demolition, was bought by the present owners, Mr. and Mrs. R. Bullock and sympathetically restored by them.

41

He eventually compounded and paid a total sum of £52. James Massey had been listed a delinquent about three years earlier; among a number of such offenders in the Macclesfield Hundred there appears "James Massey of Sale, Esqr. – He is an inhabitant of the Bucklow Hundred".

One thing not in the Masseys' favour was an antipathy which existed between Richard, the son, and Sir William Brereton of Handforth. Brereton was the Parliamentary commander in Cheshire and one of Cromwell's ablest generals. It appears that in 1635 Richard Massey had clashed with Brereton using "provoking words and gestures", the outcome being that Massey was compelled to sign an abject apology before witnesses.

Probably James Massey did not support the Royalist cause very actively; neither he nor his son took part in the defence of Wythenshawe Hall which fell to local Parliamentary forces in 1644.

A century later the area was again the scene of military activity. In 1745 the invading Jacobite army marched south from Edinburgh into England and, by clever tactical ruses, succeeded in confusing the Government's intelligence service regarding their destination. The Government forces, therefore, were concentrated in the north midlands until it should become clear which direction the rebels were taking. Whether to the west and Wales to gain support from a rising there; or to London without delay.

Such was the speed of the Jacobites' advance into Lancashire that, in an effort to delay them, the Government ordered the Mersey bridges to be broken down. Shortly afterwards the rebels reached Manchester and, from this time Crossford Bridge became a key factor in the strategy of 'the Young Pretender' Charles Edward Stuart, for the Jacobites used it to feint a move towards Chester and the west, the obvious destination should their army leave Manchester by way of Crossford Bridge.

The rebels made a great deal of fuss repairing the bridge to ensure that Government intelligence could not fail to know about it, impressing on the Manchester constables that the work must go ahead without delay. An intelligence report from Knutsford said "the first news we had was that they were making a Bridge over the Mersey at Stretford . . . We had messengers out all night who confirmed their making of the Bridge with Poplars and Planks. Particularly the Rev. Mr. Barlow who saw the first Tree that reached over land about 3 o'clock. About 6 they effected their Design so **as to make it possible for ffoot. This was done chiefly by the Country People about Stretford whom they compelled to assist".**

The bridge, once repaired, was then used for its intended purpose. A small force of rebels, having crossed it, made for Sale and Altrincham, and another intelligence report said that "at Sale Moor [they] were met by the 12 Dragoons, the officer was an old Man and courageous, standing his ground till the Enemy was very near and then retreated and went back to Congleton to give information to the Regiment who marched . . . immediately to Newcastle".

42

Plate 10: The building shown here is an example of the ultimate in vernacular architecture and was possibly designed by the tenant-farmer for whom it was built, unlike the 17th century house on Cross Street and the 18th century double-pile house at the corner of Wythenshawe Road, both of which conform to vernacular building styles of their period; the latter building having its front elevation constructed in the fashionable Flemish bond of the time.

The building illustrated here however, situated near Rutland Lane and built about the same time, is constructed largely in modified English or garden-wall bond of about five courses of stretchers to one of headers.

The building is described in 1806 as a house and barn occupied by Robert Marsland and Peter Carshaw and was in occupation until the 1980s.

The Government troops were at Newcastle-under-Lyme, Stone, Stafford, Lichfield and Coventry in anticipation of the rebels' expected thrust to the west, and meanwhile the main force of rebels had left Manchester, crossing the Mersey at Stockport and Cheadle and were on their way to London, their advance being cut short at Derby.

In 1759, the Duke of Bridgewater obtained an Act of Parliament to construct a canal in order to carry coal from his collieries at Worsley to Salford and Hollin Ferry; in 1760 a further Act was obtained which changed the route so that the canal ran from Worsley, crossed the Irwell at Barton and proceeded to Manchester. In 1762 a third Act was passed to construct a further branch from Stretford, through Sale and Altrincham to Runcorn; although the section of the canal through Sale was completed in 1765, work was held up at Norton so that the complete waterway did not come into operation until 1776. Some years ago I came across the following advertisement in the Manchester Mercury in 1772:

WANTED, Immediately,
FORTY or FIFTY good LABOURING MEN, to
Work in Trafford Meadows, within three Miles
of Manchester, Cutting for the Navigation.
Those that can Work well, will meet with great
Encouragement, as there is a Foreman to set
them to Work, and all Materials found them.

This advertisement is rather puzzling as the part of the canal in Trafford meadows would belong to the section opened in 1765. Dating the canal precisely is not easy, which is surprising for such a recent event in history; although the bi-centenary celebrations of the opening of the Worsley-Manchester section were held in 1961, the fact is that in 1761 the canal had only reached as far as Stretford, the coal being transported the rest of the way to Manchester by carts. As the Duke had promised, the price of coal sold in Manchester fell from 7d.(3p.) to 3½d. (1½p.)per cwt.

In 1765 a canal was proposed from Stockport and Macclesfield to the Mersey; the Duke of Bridgewater successfully opposed the Bill in the House of Lords and obtained an Act the following year for a canal from Sale to Stockport. This branch was probably never intended to be constructed, but was merely a means of thwarting the rival canal.

The branch from Stretford, through Sale and Altrincham to Runcorn, cost £220,000 but it must have given a considerable boost to the economy locally as, henceforth, the rapidly growing town of Manchester and other places could be supplied with fresh produce from north Cheshire, transported quickly and cheaply.

An embankment had to be constructed across the Mersey valley to maintain the canal at the required level and an aqueduct known as Barfoot Bridge was built to carry the canal over the Mersey. The Duke's engineer, James Brindley, mentioned in a letter

Plate 11: Brindley's aqueduct, known as Barfoot Bridge, completed about 1765. The view is of the west side of the aqueduct which carries the Bridgewater Canal over the River Mersey.

that he had calculated what height the arch of the aqueduct should be. However, in 1770, a notice appeared in the Manchester Mercury claiming damages by several Sale yeomen alleging that "the arch at Barfoot Hough is not of sufficient height and width" and, consequently, they had suffered damage to crops through flooding in 1768.

Brindley would have severe limitations imposed on him regarding the dimensions of the arch; the total height of the aqueduct was limited by the height above the river of the canal it was to carry, it must have sufficient strength to bear the weight of the water and, at the same time, the arch had to be high enough for the river to flow through when in flood. Brindley probably achieved the optimum calculation to try to satisfy all these conditions; within the imposed limits he could do no more.

On August 17, 1799, "a severe storm of wind and rain" swept away many bridges along the River Mersey and, on the following day, the river broke its bank on the Sale side east of the present railway bridge as shown on a plan drawn by Thomas Rogers in that year. As it had been feared that the embanked canal may have given way under the weight of the trapped flood water, protection was given for the future by the construction of a stone weir, over which flood water would flow along a two-mile long channel abandoned by the river centuries ago.

The weir was swept away by a flood in the summer of 1840 and another was constructed, being completed in 1841. Previous to this, heavy flooding on June 14,

Plate 12: The weir, built in 1841 to replace an earlier one.

1828 had once again broken the river bank near Barlow Hall above Jackson's Boat during hay harvest time. The water rose so rapidly that the horses had to be unharnessed from the carts and a stampede made for the nearest high ground.

The pressure of the water on the bank above Barfoot Bridge caused the bank to give way and the rush of water nearly swept away the aqueduct. To save it the nearest trees were felled; they were weighted with stones and secured by chains and, along with boats laden with straw, were sunk there. This resulted in an indictment against Thomas Joseph Trafford and others, owners of the bank. The action was brought by the Duke of Bridgewater's trustees.

In the 18th and early 19th centuries, the canal was used not only for the transporting of goods, but also for passenger traffic. The "swift packets" travelling at a speed of up to ten miles an hour, with periodic changes of horses.

"The sail from Manchester to Runcorn, in the Packet Boats, is very amusing" said a contemporary chronicler. "Strangers, on setting off from Castle Quay are surprised at the very large warehouses . . . passing Stretford, you arrive at the aqueduct over Chorlton Brook and the River Mersey, at the former place, owing to the heavy rains, a breach was made in the canal the last year; [1799] under the aqueduct is a very deep piece of water, which owing to a spring, and being three times overflowed, was found difficult to repair, but from the ingenious method of pumping by steam engines, (one of which is a floating one) it was carried into effect; passing the Mersey on the left hand, is a pretty hermitage belonging to Dr. White; on coming to Sale Moor, is a most beautiful piece of water, being so straight for two miles, that you look through three bridges, and at its extent stands the parish church of Boden, which makes a very picturesque appearance; at Altringham, the boat stops about ten minutes . . . ".

One of the stages where the horses were changed still exists on the west bank of the canal at Stretford near Brindley's aqueduct and is known as the Watch House.

All this time throughout the centuries following the Dissolution of the Monasteries, which released one-third of all the land in England onto the market, the number of small landowners and tenants in Sale as elsewhere, had been steadily growing, eventually leading to the creation of many small farms held on lease. In Cheshire, by the 18th century, most land was held by copyhold, which means that there were over-rights held by the former lord of the manor, but the tenant had virtual ownership. However, if the copyholder had no heir, the land went back to the lord. At the death of the copyholder a sum of money called the heriot was payable to the lord. This could be waived if the heir agreed to a lease for life, which meant that after a number of agreed generations, usually three, the land reverted once again to the lord.

Leases for life were commonplace in Cheshire by the end of the 18th century, although they were giving way to leases for will, where a bargain was struck between landlord and tenant producing rack rents. The rack rent was the correct legal term; under this system the rent was raised to the maximum figure that the tenant could pay and still survive. The system led to the impoverishment of the land on a wide scale and, consequently, in 1793, the Board of Agriculture was established by William Pitt.

One of the first tasks undertaken by the Board was to organise a series of reports on the various counties, regarding the state of agriculture. A draft on Cheshire was circulated in 1794 and a revised version by Henry Holland published in 1808.

According to the 1794 report Cheshire covered 676,000 statute acres, most of which was in use. The report found that there were few farms of more than 300 acres, going on to suggest that there was at least one farmer to every 80 acres. The report mentions that the diet of the agricultural labourer in Cheshire consisted chiefly of potatoes, barley bread and butter (surprisingly scarcely any cheese) butter-milk, etc.; that his winter wages were seven to eight shillings (35p to 40p) a week and nine to fifteen shillings (45p to 75p) a week in the spring months.

Marl was used as a fertiliser in Sale and elsewhere from the Middle Ages until the 19th century, although by this time night soil was generally used. The night soil was the contents of the dry lavatories or "privies" which was brought back from Manchester by the farmers of north Cheshire when they had delivered their produce to the market. The ashes from the domestic fires also went into the privies; the contents were spread on the land and anything indestructible, such as broken clay pipes, which had been thrown into the fire, survived. Therefore, the presence of pieces of clay pipestem or, less frequently, pipe bowls in garden soil is an indication of 18th or 19th century arable farming in that area.

By the beginning of the 19th century, most of the land in Sale was worked by tenant farmers and smallholders, with the exception of slightly more than 300 acres of waste known as Sale Moor; this started at Washway Road, lying betwen School

Road and what is now Raglan Road, and ran eastwards mainly north of Marsland Road, as far as the Legh Arms. It constituted about one-hundredth of the waste in the whole of Cheshire; these wastes or commons, totalling about 30,000 acres being used by the cottagers to supplement their subsistence living by grazing a cow or other animal on them. The Board of Agriculture recommended that the waste in Cheshire be enclosed and brought into cultivation.

Sources for Chapter 4 – Sale before the Enclosure Act

Christopher Saxton's map of Cheshire, 1577.

P. P. Burdett's map of Cheshire, 1777.

Map of estates in Sale of G. J. Legh, 1801.

Owen MSS. vol. 19.

William Yates's map of Lancashire, 1786.

Dore, R. N. The Early Life of Sir William Brereton. Transactions Lancashire and Cheshire Antiquarian Society, vol. 63, 1952–3.

Transactions Lancashire and Cheshire Antiquarian Society, vol. 68, 1958.

Manchester Mercury. June 16, 1772; September 15, 1772; July 10, 1770.

Bancks's Manchester and Salford Directory, 1800.

General View of the Agriculture of Cheshire, 1794.

Plate 13: The building shown here nos. 118-120 Cross Street, dating from the late 17th century, is Sale's oldest known building, constructed from 2½ inch (60mm) thick brick and having, in common with other similar examples in the region, relieving arches to divert some of the load from door and window openings; the latter originally having wooden mullions.

Like many vernacular brick buildings of the period the upper floor is in one respect over-engineered with unnecessarily heavy beams; it is generally accepted that these were to help support the walls, the local builders of small houses only just emerging from timber-frame construction and unsure of the capabilities of brick walls. However, in this house a beam of 12 ins (300mm) square section has one end supported only by a window lintel.

The reason for the use of such heavy timbers in vernacular buildings, in some cases at least, may be due to an availability at the time of cheap used timber from medieval timber-frame houses demolished during the Great Rebuilding (1670-1720 in the north). One floor beam of 10 ins (250mm) square section has short joists placed on edge jointed into both sides of the beam; but there is evidence that the beam originally had joists threaded through it which were placed flat in accordance with medieval timber-frame construction practise.

5

The Enclosure and
the Tithes

Part of the moor or common in Sale was enclosed by agreement among the landowners during the 17th century, as mentioned in an earlier chapter. In the 18th and early 19th centuries a different type of enclosure took place; this was enclosure by Act of Parliament, each district involved having a separate Act of Parliament to carry the enclosure through in a methodical way. In some areas of the country, the enclosures included open-field arable, still surviving from feudal times; but in Cheshire only commons and wastes were involved.

The enclosure of the commons served several purposes. At the time that most of them took place Britain was at war with France and food imports from the Continent had virtually ceased. The bringing of the commons into cultivation meant that more food could be produced profitably, as food prices were high. Another factor was that people who had taken to living on the common were a constant thorn in the side of the landowners and had been since the end of the feudal system. As one reporter for the Board of Agriculture in the west country remarked, "Let those who doubt go round the commons now open, and view the miserable huts, and poor, ill-cultivated, impoverished spots erected, or rather thrown together . . . which . . . affords them a very trifle towards their maintenance, yet operates upon their minds as a sort of independence; this idea leads the man to lose many days' work, by which he gets a habit of indolence; a daughter kept at home to milk a poor half starv'd cow, who being open to temptations soon turns harlot, and becomes a distrest ignorant mother instead of making a good useful servant".

Whether or not people lived on the common in Sale is not known; it is possible, as the number of permanent buildings in Sale shown on the 1806 map does not look sufficient to house a population recorded as 819 in 1801. On the other hand, if people lived on the common before the enclosure, where did they live afterwards? There is no indication of cottages built in significant numbers in the following years and, although there is evidence that some moved to the towns for employment, the number could not have been considerable for, by 1811, the population had increased to 911.

Because these were Parliamentary enclosures the rights vested in the inhabitants of a district by an Enclosure Award are law to this day and can only be abolished by Act of Parliament. This was demonstrated in 1961 at the Court of Appeal, when it was held that the inhabitants of Wraysbury, Bucks., were entitled to hold an annual fair on a plot of land which had been allotted for that purpose by the Enclosure Award of Wraysbury of 1803. A builder had bought the land for building purposes, but four inhabitants sought to preserve the ancient right and won the case.

From feudal times the peasant had guarded his rights on the common to cut turf, gather fuel, pasture a cow, etc., but the enclosure of the common brought these rights to an end. On February 8, 1805 the Sale Enclosure Petition was presented to the House of Commons, stating that "there is in the Township of Sale, in the County Palatine of Chester, a certain Common called Sale Moor, and other Waste Lands; and if the same were divided and enclosed, it would be very advantageous to all Persons therein . . .".

Divided and enclosed meant that the common was to be divided up amongst the people who owned land in Sale in proportion to the size of their holdings. For example, a landowner having 100 acres could expect a share of the common twice that of someone who owned 50 acres. After the division, each allotment was enclosed with a hawthorn hedge.

Commissioners were appointed to supervise the enclosure, and they appointed a Surveyor to carry out the work. The Commissioners appointed for Sale Moor were Josiah Potts of Oulerton, James Stelfox of High Legh and Richard Clark, or Clarke, of Ashley. The Surveyor was Edward Mason of Chorlton.

On March 4, 1805 a petition of "several Persons interested in a certain Moor, called Sale Moor . . ." was presented to the House of Commons. It stated that the Bill for enclosure contained "divers powers and provisions, which will, if passed into law, be very prejudicial to the rights and interests of the Petitioners . . .". On March 12, several amendments which had been made to the Bill were read out twice and agreed to by the House.

The Bill was read for the third time on March 14 and was passed and sent to the Lords. On April 1, it was reported that the Lords had passed the Bill with some amendments (usually the Lords' amendments were trivial) and these were agreed to by the Commons on April 2; the Bill receiving Royal Assent on April 5, 1805; its purpose being to enclose "a certain Common called Sale Moor . . . containing . . . One Hundred and fifty-two Acres after the Rate of Eight Yards to the Rod or Perch commonly called Cheshire Measure".

This is a suitable point at which to consider briefly the origins of the Cheshire Measure, or Cheshire Acre as it is usually called, the largest of the acres. In the Anglo-Saxon period the measurements of land were subjective rather than objective; in other words based on what the land would produce and this varied from one area to another.

The oldest Anglo-Saxon unit of land was the hide which meant a piece of land, some arable, some pasture, sufficient to support a certain type of family. Naturally, in an area of highly productive land, the hide would be smaller than in an area of poorer land. The hide was divided into quarters or virgates and eighths or oxgangs, there was an average of 100 to 120 acres to the hide; consequently, the size of the acre was in direct relation to the size of the hide.

This system continued well into the Middle Ages, the acre alone finally becoming a fixed unit of measurement, constant within a given county when production for subsistence gave way to production for market. Therefore, the acre and its subdivisions survived; the Cheshire acre being 2.1 times that of a statute acre.

The total area of Sale Moor would be something over 300 statute acres; this included roads, watering places as some of the ponds or pits were designated and slightly over 279 acres divided into allotments and enclosed. Notice of the time and place of the first meeting of the Commissioners was "affixed upon the outer door" of St. Martin's Church and was also advertised in Wheeler's Manchester Chronicle; the meeting being held at the Unicorn in Altrincham. Anyone claiming rights of soil or other rights on the common was required to attend and present their claims in writing.

A second and third meeting was held at the Unicorn on May 29 and June 24, 1805, followed by a number of further meetings. The people who either appeared personally, or were represented as claimants to common or other rights on Sale Moor were: —

"*William Egerton and George John Legh as owners of the soil of the said Common and waste lands and as owners and proprietors of divers lands tenements and hereditaments within the said Township of Sale and the said George Harry, Earl of Stamford and Warrington, Charles White, Lawrence Wright, Joseph Atkinson, George Ashton, John Moore, William Whitelegg (of Northen), Henry Baxter and Peter Howard, and also Rebecca Baker, Hannah Scholefield, James Marsland, Ralph Barlow, Joseph Warburton (for and on behalf of his son John Warburton), Edward Gratrix, Timothy Leigh, Lucy Jewsbury, William Williamson, John Carver, The Rev. Richard Popplewell Johnson (as Patron and Rector . . . in respect of the Glebe lands belonging to the said Rectory), Hugh Creasty, James Hunt, James Renshaw, John Cookson, John Heywood, Samuel Barlow, William Morris, John Whitehead, Sir John Thorold (for and on behalf of his wife Lady Jane Thorold). Thomas Hesketh, The Trustees of the real estates late of William Davenport deceased, Joseph Taylor, Edward Astley, John Moore (as Trustee of Hannah Cheetham), Richard Pearson, Peter Hulme, William Whitelegg (of Cross Street), John Royle (of Cross Street), John Higson, John Marsland, George Williamson, Robert Barlow, Ralph Ashton, Margaret Peers (alias Margaret Pearson), Jonathan Davenport, Elizabeth Whitwell (as Mortgagee in possession of certain lands and hereditaments in Sale aforesaid late belonging to John Davenport deceased), John Royle (of Sale), William Roylance and Thomas Woodall*".

Objections to Claims

Elizabeth Whitwell's claim as mortgagee "in possession of the Cottages lands and hereditaments . . ." was also included wholly or in part "in the several claims of the said Charles White, John Whitehead and Jonathan Davenport . . .". Charles White objected in writing to the Commissioners at the third meeting; but as his objection was to the claim of the deceased Jonathan Davenport and did not dispute the claim of Elizabeth Whitwell as a mortgagee of the respective land etc., the Commissioners allotted to Elizabeth Whitwell such shares as they considered she was entitled to.

Claims Given Up

William Morris, John Higson, John Royle (of Sale) and William Roylance claimed right of common and shares and allotments respecting land etc. held under George John Legh by lease for life. George John Legh also claimed right of common upon and shares and allotments regarding the same land. John Higson, John Royle and William Roylance then withdrew their claims. Legh did not object to the claim of William Morris, so the Commissioners set out and allotted to William Morris such parts shares or allotments as, in their judgment, he was entitled to in respect of the land he held under lease.

Henry Baxter claimed land etc. occupied by James Hulme and Elizabeth Pearson respectively, which he claimed had been seized by them; and also certain other land and property also in the occupation of James Hulme, to which Henry Baxter claimed to be entitled during the term of the life of Elizabeth Pearson, widow, and which Richard Pearson claimed to be entitled to the fee simple after her death. Henry Baxter withdrew his claim to the last mentioned land etc., and requested the Commissioners to assign it to Richard Pearson, which they did.

William Egerton had lately died, leaving his eldest living son, Wilbràham, (William Tatton the eldest son having died without issue during William Egerton's lifetime) so that Wilbraham Egerton became, in the opinion of the Commissioners, along with George John Legh, entitled to the "rights of soil of the said Common and waste lands and the mines minerals marl clay sand and gravel lying and being within and under the same no objection having been made before us the said Commissioners to the claims of the said Wilbraham Egerton and George John Legh to be owners of the said Common and waste lands nor any other person or persons other than and except the said Wilbraham Egerton and George John Legh having claimed to be owner or owners thereof".

Sales Made

Wilbraham Egerton to John Moore: Right of soil in respect of 7a. 2r. 3p. and 2a. 1r. 29p.

Wilbraham Egerton to John Whitehead: Right of soil in respect of 3a. 2r. 20p.

Wilbraham Egerton to William Morris: Right of soil in respect of 7a. 0r. 29p.

Margaret Peers (alias Pearson) to Charles White Esquire: Right of common in respect of cottage and premises in her possession.

George Ashton to James Hope – Bricksetter: Right of common in respect of "four several Cottages and Gardens and a Croft thereto belonging".

James Renshaw to John Moore: "Right title and interest shares and allotments of in and to the said Common and waste lands by virtue of the claim made by him . . .".

John Warburton to James Clarke – Shoemaker: "Right title . . . as before".

John Marsland to Edward Marsland – Yeoman: "Right title . . ." (with the exception of a certain portion).

Ralph Barlow to Robert Barlow – Cordwainer: "Right title . . .".

John Garner to Thomas Woodall: "Right title . . ." (with the exception of a certain portion).

Exchanges

Charles White Esquire and James Marsland: White exchanged 4a. 2r. 10p. and 1a. 2r. 19¼p. for a parcel of meadow land.

Charles White Esquire and Thomas Woodall: White exchanged 1a. 3r. 13p. for a parcel of meadow land.

John Astley and James Marsland: Astley exchanged 4a. 2r. 32p. for "part of the moor field and 24p.".

Jonathan Davenport had died and his heir was allotted what Jonathan Davenport would have been entitled to.

An allotment was made for gravel pits for repairing roads and another for the Trustees of the canal to take stone, sand etc. for the maintenance of same. These allotments were each one Cheshire acre, and the herbage of them was to be the property of the freeholders of the Township of Sale. A further allotment was made for a School House. The first six crops of corn or grain which were grown on Sale Moor after the passing of the Act were to be free of Tithes.

All costs and charges incurred by the surveying, planning, alloting etc. and by the making of drains and roads were to be borne in a proportionate Rate by all the proprietors or owners of allotments. It was made an offence to graze cattle of any sort on any of the roads or ways made by virtue of the Act "and which shall be made into roads or lanes and fenced on both sides after the passing of the Act; nor shall any person for the space of seven years after the passing of the Act, graze or keep sheep or lambs on any of the allotments unless he folds the same, or guard the young quickset hedges adjoining his allotment".

Boundaries

The Common and waste lands to be enclosed were bounded by "ancient inclosed lands" and by the Turnpike Road from Crossford Bridge to Altrincham.

Roads

The Commissioners set out and appointed "public carriage roads and highways through and over the said Common and waste lands" also "such private roads or ways watercourses and watering places in over upon and through or by the sides of the allotments". There were two public roads 40ft. (12.2 metres) wide exclusive of ditches; one "leading from Northen (otherwise Northenden) ... over Marsland Bridge" to the "Turnpike Road leading from Crossford Bridge to Altrincham". The other following the present-day line of School Road and Northenden Road.

Nine more public roads were appointed; these being 30ft. (9 metres) wide exclusive of ditches. For example, to give them the names by which we know them, Old Hall Road, Baguley Road and Temple Road and one extending "the ancient public road or highway called Broad Lane" to the canal bridge.

There were twelve private roads 18ft. (5.5 metres) wide exclusive of ditches. One led from Northenden Road, near Gratrix Lane, to two cottages in the possession of Edmund Royle and Esther Hurlbert. The road and the "bridges or platts thereon" had to be maintained by the owners and occupiers of the two cottages. There were also two private roads 12ft. (3.6 metres) wide exclusive of ditches, and one private road 24ft. (7.3 metres) wide exclusive of ditches.

Three drains or watercourses were set out on the "Common and waste lands". These were 6ft. (1.8 metres) in width at the surface of the ground. Drain no. 1 ran from "the ancient watercourse" near Derbyshire Road (I am here using the modern names of the roads) under Wardle Road and pursued a straight course into the canal. Drain no. 2 ran from drain no. 1 parallel with and between Wardle Road and the canal, under Marsland Road and into "the ancient watercourse there running between ancient inclosed lands belonging to the said William Williamson and the close called the poorhouse Croft". The "ancient watercourse" we know as Baguley Brook. Drain no. 3 ran from the westerly side of the canal to Washway Road and "through a culvert made across the said Turnpike Road by the Trustees of the same road into the ancient watercourse there". The culvert was about midway between School Road and Marsland road.

Watering Places

The Commissioners appointed six "watering places". No. 1 lay on the easterly side of Washway Road some distance from, and on the Altrincham side of, Marsland Road. No. 2 seems to have consisted of two ponds or pools, one close to Derbyshire Road, the other close to Marsland Road. Both being on the westerly side of the junction of the two roads. No. 3 lay ·on the north side of Northenden Road, about midway between Wythenshawe Road and Baguley Road. No. 4 was on the east side of Wythenshawe Road and the south side of New Hall Road right at the junction of the two roads and directly opposite what older people knew as the "marl pit school", demolished some years ago. No. 5 was situated on the north side of Broad Road, between Temple Road and Old Hall Road and, finally, no. 6 lay on the west side of Temple Road, not far from Northenden Road.

All these watering places lay close to the roadway and so were easily accessible so that they "may be used and enjoyed by the inhabitants of the said Township of Sale and by all persons whomsoever as and for public watering places".

A coal wharf is marked on the Enclosure map, with a "new warehouse" to the north of it and a timber yard to the south in the vicinity of the present railway station.

On June 20, 1807, the Commissioners called a meeting at the Bull's Head in Cross Street in order to read out the Enclosure Award. Sale Moor, as an open space, received what amounted to a great send-off in 1804, the year previous to the passing of the Enclosure Act, when 6,000 Volunteers and regular troops, comprising cavalry, infantry and artillery drawn from various towns in south Lancashire and north Cheshire, held a review on the common; a full account is given in Cheshire Notes and Queries vol. 5, 1900.

The watering places appointed by the Commissioners were ponds, most of which will have been former gravel or marl pits which had filled with water. Water no. 1 was bounded by Washway Road and what later became Raglan Road and Sale Heys Road. The plot of land partly occupied by the pit was known, colloquially, as Adam's Vineyard. This was a jocular name; just as drinking water was sometimes referred to as Adam's ale by an earlier generation, so this pond was Adam's vineyard. I mention this so that anyone doing research on 19th century Sale will not imagine that there was ever a vineyard in this unsuitable area. The pond was filled in later in the 19th century and a horse-trough placed nearby; the site now being occupied by the Baptist church.

The tithe was the ancient obligation of each parishioner to pay one-tenth of his produce to the incumbent of the parish. In the case of Ashton and Sale this was a rector, therefore he received the great tithe, unlike a vicar, part of whose tithe went to the bishop of the diocese. The General View of the Agriculture of Cheshire, 1794, referring to the tithes stated "The present impolitic and, in many cases, oppressive mode of collecting tithes in kind is one of the obstacles to general improvements". The report urged the Board to consider a plan for the commutation of the tithes; in other words the Board was in favour of a change from handing over one-tenth of the actual produce to the payment of a fixed sum of money. Incidentally, it is interesting to note how the meaning of the word "commute" has changed in the second half of the 20th century with its frequent misuse of words. A commuter was formerly someone who travelled regularly using a railway season ticket. The payment of a separate fare for each journey had been commuted to a fixed payment for a period; but now the term is used to describe anyone who travels daily to work, whatever his mode of transport.

On April 20, 1844 a Tithe Award was made for Sale. The Enclosure Award, of 1807 shows that the area of Sale totalled slightly more than 2,204 statute acres, while the tithes in 1844 were commuted on the basis of 1,866 acres. The reason for this discrepancy is that some land already paid a rent charge to the Rector in lieu of tithes. One estate estimated at about 182 acres was free of the render of the tithe of hay by an annual payment of fourteen shillings (70p); another estate of 148 acres also paid an annual rent charge instead of rendering hay and the Rector held 10 acres of glebe land, that is land held by the parish church, and this of course was free of tithes.

The land covered by the Tithe Award consisted of 1,300 acres of arable, 500 acres of meadow and 30 acres of woodland and so it can be seen the emphasis had changed to arable farming. Oats were most commonly grown, followed by barley and then wheat. The total annual rent charge payable to the Rector from the land in Sale covered by the Tithe Award was slightly more than £489.

From the Enclosure and Tithe Awards it can be determined whether the shift in the years 1807–44 was towards fewer landowners with larger holdings or the reverse. In 1807 there were 52 proprietors of land in Sale with a total holding of about 2,000 acres in the township and former common; at least half of the total being owned by four persons. George John Legh and Wilbraham Egerton owned more than 420 acres between them; The Earl of Stamford and Warrington more than 300 acres; Charles White more than 290 acres. Of the remainder Lawrence Wright had over 150 acres; eight proprietors had between 30 and 100 acres each; about 20 owned between 5 and 30 acres leaving a further 20 people each having less than 5 acres.

By 1844 the position had changed considerably. The number of landowners had increased from 52 in 1807 to 90. George Cornwall Legh owned more than 185 acres; Mary Woodwise more than 100 acres; John White more than 290 acres; Lawrence Wright more than 150 acres. Fifteen people owned between 30 and 100 acres each; about 25 owned between 5 and 30 acres and 46 proprietors, including the trustees of the Primitive Methodist, Wesleyan Methodist, and Independent Chapels, owned less than 5 acres.

The proportion of landowners compared with population remained virtually the same. The population of Sale in 1807 would be about 850 and in 1844 about 1,500, in both cases amounting to about 1/17 of the population. It will be seen that the losses

1807		1844	
Landowners	Acreage	Landowners	Acreage
3	more than 250	1	more than 250
1	100–250	3	100–250
8	30–100	15	30–100
20	5–30	25	5–30
20	under 5	46	under 5
Total 52	2,000	Total 90	2,000

have occurred among the bigger landowners, the greatest gains being made among the class owning less than 5 acres.

This can perhaps be partly explained by the fact that in 1829, 515 acres, or a quarter of the township passed by sale to Samuel Brooks of Manchester, from Lord Stamford and others. It seems probable that Brooks bought out Stamford and Egerton, neither name appearing in the 1844 list. By that year Brooks had sold well over 400 acres.

Sale remained a predominantly agricultural area well into the 19th century. In 1811 the proportion of families engaged in agricultural occupations was about the average for the Bucklow Hundred. In the Hundred as a whole there were 3,034 families in agriculture and 2,562 in industry. The figures for Sale in the same period are 92 families engaged in agriculture and 67 families engaged in trade, manufacture, or handicraft. These figures may be contrasted to those of Altrincham where there were only 82 families in agriculture compared to 276 families in industry.

Sources for Chapter 5 – The Enclosure and the Tithes

Sale Enclosure map, 1806.

House of Commons Journals. February 8; March 4, 11, 1805.

Wheeler's Manchester Chronicle. June 20, 1807.

Sale Moor Enclosure Award, 1807.

Sale Township Minutes.

Sale Tithe Award, 1844.

Census returns, 1811.

a. acre   r. rood   p. perch

6

Social Conditions after the Enclosure Act

On the national scale the poor constituted the bulk of the population in the late 18th and early 19th centuries as indicated by the contemporary term the "labouring poor". It was the period when the factory system which, in the longer term, was to give the industrialised nations of the world a standard of life undreamed of by our ancestors but, in the period dealt with here meant, for those employed in the factories, a hard working day of from fourteen hours upwards, six days a week throughout the year except for Christmas Day and Good Friday.

These conditions led to outbreaks of violence in the midlands and north particularly in 1811–1812, known as the Luddite Riots after the leader, Ned Ludd, who organised the smashing of machines. Among their demands was that the State should enforce existing laws for the fair regulation of wages and hours as, under the same laws, combinations or trade unions were illegal and this part of the law was enforced. The alarm felt by the propertied class was present not only in the manufacturing towns, but in the countryside also, where bands of semi-starving labourers were committing acts of arson as a means of protest. The unease of the landowners in Sale is reflected in entries in the Sale township minutes of the time.

There were a number of reasons for the poverty in the rural areas; one was high food prices due to the Napoleonic wars; cottage industry was in decline, the standard of living of the handloom weaver being driven down by the increasing number of mills and a third factor in some areas was the enclosure of the commons, which deprived the labourers of their customary rights to pasture an animal, as the common no longer existed.

As a result of the enclosure of the commons, large numbers of labourers were forced to seek work in the manufacturing towns and, arguably, it can be said that but for the enclosures, the Industrial Revolution may not have taken place in England at the time it did or, at least, not on the same scale. A worse place of employment than the factory was the workhouse; a number of parishes could combine in a "union" to erect a workhouse which was then hired out to a manufacturer who employed as many of the jobless poor of the Union as could be accommodated; Sale was in the Altrincham Union.

Before dealing with poor relief in Sale, it may be as well to look at some contemporary observations on the condition of the poor generally in order to provide a background from which to look at events in Sale. Although some caution should be used as conditions in our area were not necessarily as severe as those described. A report in the Observer of March 17, 1816 reads as follows:—

"State of the Nation. The Duke of Bedford in the course of a lengthened and eloquent appeal to their Lordships upon this subject, adverted in the following terms to the distresses of the country; 'In many places the land was out of cultivation. Upon two estates in Norfolk, land was offered to tenants free, if they would cultivate them, but none would take them. The jails were crowded with people, unable to bear up against the pressures of the times. The farmers were imprisoned for debt, and the poorer classes, unable to procure subsistence in a legal way, became robbers of farm-yards: and the whole of the landed interest was in a condition horrible to think of . . .'".

Again, on August 11, 1816 the Observer reported "The most frightful details of the misery of the starving population are daily appearing. In some parts, it seems that bread is become a luxury and that the herbs of the fields and other indigestable substances are swallowed to appease the gnawing of hunger . . .".

The records of poor relief in Sale begin in 1808, the year following the Enclosure Award and, in the early years, are mainly claims for money for rent, or straightforward relief. In 1812, at the height of the Luddites' agitation, a special effort was made to provide potatoes for the poor in Sale; it is also apparent that there was a certain amount of unrest in this area at the time.

To quote from the minutes of the township meeting of April 27, 1812:

"At a meeting of the principal inhabitants of the Township of Sale held this Day at the New School to take into consideration the best method of affording Relief to the honest and industrious Poor of the said Township, the following Resolutions were unanimously agreed to.

1st   That a Subscription be immediately entered into and that the Amount thereof be applied to the purchasing (of) potatoes.

2nd   That as it is desirable to encourage the Cultivation of Potatoes during the present Season as much as possible those poor Persons who can procure Land shall receive a Quantity of Potatoes gratis in proportion to the Manure which they have.

3rd   That the industrious Poor of the said Township shall receive Potatoes according to the Number of their Families at half price.

4th   That a Committee of ten of the Subscribers be chosen for the purpose of purchasing and distributing the Potatoes, two of whom shall be the Overseers of the Poor, and that in order to prevent any improper Applications, two or more of the said Number shall personally examine into the state of the Poor and shall apportion the Quantity to be so distributed.

5th   That this Meeting feels for the present sufferings of the Poor and wishing to afford them all proper Relief does most highly disapprove of asking Charity by going from House to House in Numbers, and that all Persons doing so or using any expressions tending to inflame or make uneasy the Minds of their Neighbours will be excluded from any Benefit of the above Subscription in the Distribution of which regard will be had to the Character of the Applicants.

6th That this meeting does particularly recommend it to the Publicans in the Neighbourhood to allow no improper tippling in their Houses but to shut them at 10 o'Clock in the Evening to discourage all Conversation tending to inflame the public Mind, and as it is suspected that evil disposed Persons are travelling about the Country, to excite a Spirit of Discontent and Uneasiness, they are requested to be particularly watchful of all Strangers who may enter their Houses.

7th Such persons as prefer giving potatoes to Money shall have the option of doing so at the Market Price".

Plate 14: This end cottage, one of a group of four in Derbyshire Road built probably in the 1820s, is the only one to remain unspoilt externally. The glazing bars in the upper fixed portion of the horizontally sliding sash windows acknowledge the fashionable "Gothick" of the late Georgian period. Later in the 19th century the two middle cottages were converted into a smithy which, later still, reverted to cottages again. Although in this period the vertical sliding sash window was more usual, the horizontally sliding sash was often used for cheapness in small houses and it has a longer ancestry than the vertical, first appearing in England towards the end of the 16th century. Although most small houses of this period in Sale were built entirely in a vernacular style, these cottages bowed to the prevailing fashion.

The applications for poor relief of October 25, 1813 are typical of those to be found in the minutes and show that several persons had gone to Manchester and Stockport for employment. Although now living elsewhere, their own parish was still responsible for the payment of relief up to one year; consequently, the Overseers at their new place of abode usually returned them, temporarily at least, to their own parish just before the year had ended, otherwise they would become the responsibility of the parish to which they had moved. The entries are as follows:—

John Royle of Manchester wants some Relief he being out of work	*Granted 10/- (50p).*
Two children of Mary Brownhills, who live at their Grandfathers, are in want of Clogs and Shirts	*Granted*
Ann Moor has again applied for her rent to be considered next meeting	
Thos. Hamnett of Stockport wants some further Relief towards his Rent he continuing sick lives near the Jolly Hatters Milgate, Stockport	*Granted £1 to be visited by the Overseer*
Willm. Royle wants Clothing for his Wife and children	*To be viewed by the Overseer and report next meeting*
Phoebe Bury is to continue to have a shilling (5p) per Week till further orders to be lodged in the Hands of the Overseer towards his Rent	
Thos. Leigh wants ½ Years Rent. £3	
Hugh Davenport wants something towards maintaining a Child of his Daughter's which she had by John Garner of Timperley	*The Overseer to see the Man and examine into the Affair*
Edwd. Hamnett wants £3 to have a Boy of Sarah Brownhill's Apprentice for 7 Years, Boys name Wm. Son of John and Sarah Brownhill. John Brownhill is dead	*Granted*
Josh. Sidally wants his Rent paid say £4–10–0 (£4.50) and a Bed so that he may remove to another House nearer to the Place where he is employed Mr. Tisseck St. Mary's Gate Shoe Warehouse	

At the meeting of February 26, 1821, Jas. Williamson applied for rent 16/- (80p). It was agreed that the rent be paid provided he would agree to stop 6d. (2½p) per week from his wages and it was resolved that the Overseers of the Poor, John Hulbert and William Cookson, should make the next meeting a special meeting to consider discontinuing the payment of rents of paupers. In the event only two ley-payers attended the next meeting and so the matter was not discussed.

There were several possible reasons for the poor attendance. Most of the ley-payers were small tenant farmers, barely existing themselves due to the difficult circumstances of the time. If it had been agreed at the meeting that the payment of rents be discontinued then, knowing full well that the tenants of the cottages many of them let, could not afford to pay the rent which averaged about £5 a year, they would have the option of either allowing the tenant to fall into permanent arrears or evicting him; neither prospect being welcome.

On the other hand, if the small tenant farmers voted against the proposal, then they risked offending their landlords; the simplest solution was to stay away from the meeting. It may have been due to the failure to carry through their rents policy that the principal landowners later that year succeeded in having a magistrate approve the appointment of a Select Vestry for Sale consisting of the principal ley-payers only, in order to conduct "the Care and Management of the Poor".

At the Select Vestry's first meeting on September 24, 1821, a small amount of relief was granted to three applicants and, in December of that year, it was resolved that the meeting consent to a contract made between the Overseers of the Poor of Blackley "for the lodging, maintaining and employing" the poor of Sale, and the Overseers of the Poor of Sale and that they be authorised to complete such contracts for the future. In other words, from that time onward, the poor of Sale were to be sent to whichever workhouse could take them, or as many of them as possible.

However, this did not entirely solve the problem, as it is recorded in the Ashton-on-Mersey minute book that, at a meeting held on June 19, 1826, "for the purpose of taking into Consideration what Steps it would be most advisable to take, to relieve the distress under which the Unemployed Poor in this Parish are now labouring" it had been decided that "as it appears from a statement presented by the Churchwardens to this Meeting, of the condition of the Poor of this Parish, many of them are labouring under considerable distress, occasioned by the present commercial embarrasment and difficulty which prevails in this country, a public subscription be immediately entered into for their relief.

That the Churchwardens be requested to go from house to house throughout the Parish to collect subscriptions". It was recommended that the subscriptions for the two townships (Ashton and Sale) be kept separately. It was considered preferable to organise this subscription rather than make "additional calls on the poor's rate". The meeting was adjourned "for the purpose of naming a committee of Management for each of the two Townships and of arranging the mode of distribution".

At a meeting held the following week, it was decided that a committee for Ashton and one for Sale be formed. The Sale committee consisted of the Rector, Curate and ten ley-payers. It was resolved that "as it is probable that the Poor will be Employ'd during the Hay and Corn Harvests . . . distributions do not take place before they are ended . . .".

It is clear that the problem of poverty and the relief of it still had to be faced by the ley-payers; by allowing a Select Vestry to administer poor relief they had gained nothing and had lost their right to have a personal voice in the affairs of the poor.

A meeting of November 27, 1826 headed Subscriptions for the Poor, resolved that every subscriber of 2/6d. (12½p) should be entitled to one ticket to that amount in proportion to his subscription. That a sum not exceeding a quarter of the subscription would be paid out in the purchase of blankets. That a sum not exceeding a quarter be spent on coal. Another sum not exceeding a quarter be used to purchase potatoes.

At the next meeting held on December 11, it was ordered that this last sum be used to buy blankets and that the Treasurer complete the order for the purchase of blankets to the value of £20 "so that they may be distributed on Friday next at 1 O'clock P.M.". It was ordered that the appropriation of the remainder of the sum be left undetermined.

On December 15, it was resolved that "At the allowing of coals and blankets this day, it appearing that the wants of the poor would be best applied by an addition to the quantity of blankets and coals, ordered that the Treasurer be requested to purchase 30 pairs of blankets at 12/- [60p] per pair and also a boat load of coals, Wt. 10 tons, to be distributed on Friday the 22nd inst.".

Conditions do not appear to have improved through 1827 and 1828. In 1826, moves were started to have the canal assessed for the poor rate and, after some litigation, an assessment was agreed with the Trustees of the canal in 1828.

On March 3, 1828, it was resolved that "such aged and infirm persons belonging to the Township of Sale, as are receiving regular weekly pay at the rate of 3/- [15p] per week be reduced to 2/- [10p] per week after the 12th of next May with the option of residing in the Poor house . . . That from and after this date, no relief be allowed to any poor person who keeps a dog".

There was money for other purposes, however. At the same meeting a committee was formed to solicit a subscription to the amount of £10 "to be presented to Jno. Hulbert, assistant overseer of the poor for his laudable and indefatigable exertions in obtaining a confirmation of the Assessment to the poor's rate" made upon the trustees of the canal; and, on October 27 John Hulbert was to receive his £10 in the form of "a Silver Cup with an appropriate inscription upon it to be presented to him at the Bull's Head on the 14th of Novr. next" at a dinner to be paid for by a "considerable balance" remaining over the £10.

It was inevitable that crime would be widespread in the country under such conditions; not the evil acts of almost casual violence practised for enjoyment such as we have today. Most violence was against property, carried out by people driven beyond endurance; but the greater number of crimes involved theft, very often of food in the shape of growing produce or game.

In 1807, a Society for the Prosecution of Felons was in existence in Sale; a meeting having been called on April 6 of that year to examine the treasurer's accounts. The Society had at that time twelve members who owned or, in the case of one, tenanted one-third of the land in Sale. The annual meeting was held on April 27 and the rules agreed.

At the Township meeting held on November 22, 1808, William Leebridge, a member of the Society at that time, was directed to prosecute William Leigh for stealing potatoes belonging to William Leebridge, at the expense of the Society and a reward of 5 guineas (£5.25) was offered for the conviction of any other person involved.

In 1812 it was decided to draw up new regulations for the Society for the Prosecution of Felons and a meeting was held on July 6, 1812 "in consequence of the Recommendation of the Magistrates to form an Association for the Protection of Property and Preservation of the Peace". This Association would be in the control of the magistrates.

It was decided that the Society for the Prosecution of Felons should form a branch of the Association and that the expenses of the Association be paid from the Poor Rate, and that it was one of the objects of the Association to call the members together and to raise an alarm if necessary; every Constable should be provided with a rattle and "it be recommended to every considerable Farm House to have one". And so the Society still functioned under a different name, the important difference being that instead of it being self-financing with subscriptions from the members as previously, it was now funded from the Poor Rate.

There are a few references in the minutes to prosecutions made by the Society without always referring to the nature of the offences, but theft and damage to property occurred throughout the early years of the 19th century. On July 28, 1817, it was agreed "that to prevent Depredations a number of Hand Bills shall be printed and posted up in different Places offering a Reward to be given to any Person who will give Information of any Person committing Depredations in the Township".

This produced at least one result. The meeting of August 28, 1817 records that "Thos. Leigh saw Margaret Cotterell getting Potatoes in John Cookson's Field near the Road about 10 O'clock . . . at Night . . . she rund into the Wheat and he ran after her . . . she said 'do not tell' . . . she said she only wanted a Mess" (meal).

Three months earlier Margaret Cotterell had applied for relief and was granted 2/- (10p) "for a Week or 2". She did not apply for relief again until November 24 and was refused, her next application being five weeks later when she was granted 2/- for a few weeks.

On September 2, 1818 "It was unanimously resolved. That this meeting consider the wanton and malicious damage done to the young Timber Trees belonging to the

Earl of Stamford and Warrington and to the young fruit trees belonging to Mr. Heald and John Moore Esq. as a disgrace to the Township and that no pains or expense shall be spared to bring the Offenders to Speedy Justice". This meeting was attended by 39 people; at the previous three township meetings to consider applications for relief only four attended each time. Even at a meeting the same year called to decide future policy concerning the school only 15 were present.

Other offences included several cases of husbands deserting their families. On August 27, 1821, Lucy Graham applied for rent and for 3/- [15p] as temporary relief. As it is not recorded that anything was granted, it must be assumed that nothing was; the minutes would be used to check the expenditure. Three weeks later, it was recorded that John Graham had "forsaken his family . . . the overseer to apply to a magistrate for a warrant and offer 2 guineas [£2.10] for his apprehension . . .". John Graham appeared at the meeting of October 8 in the custody of the constable. The meeting agreed to suspend the warrant against him on the understanding tht he would move with his family into a poorhouse; he was advanced "another week's pay . . . to enable him to support his family until he gets some work out of his loom". The poorhouses were cottages owned by the township in which paupers lived rent-free; a poorhouse would often be occupied by more than one family.

The site of some of the poorhouses, the ornamental gardens at the junction of Marsland Road and Brooklands Road, is still owned by the local authority. The other poorhouses were formerly the second township school in Springfield which fell into disuse when a new school was built in about 1800; this latter school was the venue for the township meetings.

Throughout the period under discussion small farmers and businessmen were frequently bankrupted. In 1804, the Manchester Mercury advertised the auction of the premises and possessions of John Moore of Cross Street "Corn-dealer and Shop-keeper". The advertisement was addressed to John Moore's creditors and the auction included "the dwellinghouse and Warehouse . . . Household Furniture . . . malt, corn, flour, sacks, oil, cloverseed, hops, teas, sugar . . . beds, bedding and furniture, two horses, two cows, a cart and wheels, seven pigs and other stock . . .". It is possible that this is the same John Moore for which an account was paid, recorded in the township minutes of July 26, 1819, for board, etc., in the lunatic asylum in Manchester.

The township minutes, which are dealt with only briefly here, give a remarkable insight into the conditions which prevailed in Sale in the first half of the 19th century. These conditions probably persisted with slight improvement until the changes brought about by the opening of the railway in the middle of the century.

Sources for Chapter 6 – Social Conditions after the Enclosure Act

Sale Township Minutes.

Ashton-on-Mersey Township Minutes.

Manchester Mercury, August 14, 1804.

7

Education and Religion

The first school in the parish of Ashton was built in Sale in 1667 according to a feoffment, or gift, of "the schoolhouse . . . lately erected on the commons or waste lands of Sale . . . for the better education, instruction and learneing of yong children in the sayd Parrish and other places adjoyneing" by Lord Delamere, Sir Thomas Brereton, Robert Tatton, Edward Legh and Richard Massey. The schoolhouse, etc. was conveyed to Hugh Hobson, rector of the parish from 1663–79 and, thereafter, to his successors.

This was followed in 1671 by a further gift "to John Moores, garthwebweaver," by the same landowners, of a close of land enclosed from the commons, at a yearly rent of three shillings (15p) payable to the churchwardens for the use of the schoolmaster "at the now publicke schoole in Sale". The whereabouts of this first school is not known. As the only clue to its location is that it was built on the common in the 17th century, it could have been almost anywhere south of Broad Road.

The first school probably continued in use until some time in the first half of the 18th century and from then the history of the township school is much clearer due to a dispute which arose in the middle of the 19th century between the Overseers of the Poor and the rector about the future of the school. The Overseers put their case in the form of a printed pamphlet and it is from this that we learn of the origins of the second township school in Springfield and its successor in School Road. This then in a condensed form is the Overseers' case.

'*The properties belonging to the school were acquired at four different periods. The first consisted of two old cottages standing near the present school, and some land adjoining, which have been invested in the Overseers from time immemorial. It has been reported to us that two females named Barlow were the owners of these two cottages and some adjoining land. They became paupers and were supported for many years by the Overseers out of the poor rates and on their death the Overseers took possession of the cottages and land, converting the former into a school which was used as such until about 1800.*

The second acquisition consists of the present schoolhouse which was erected about 1800 by public subscription. The Duke of Bridgewater by virtue of an Act of Parliament had taken possession of and appropriated, land in the township, which was then moor or waste, for his canal, towing paths, etc. for which at the time he paid nothing, or no adequate consideration. About the year 1800 several gentlemen in Sale resolved to build a larger school in expectation that a considerable sum might be obtained from the Duke's agent. They commenced soliciting subscriptions from the public; and many gentlemen in Manchester unconnected with Sale, subscribed. They then waited upon the agent of the Duke who was induced to give them a liberal contribution, and so the school was erected, and when it was completed the original one was converted back into cottages.

The third acquisition comprised all the land and buildings now belonging to the school and this was confirmed by the Enclosure Award of June 29, 1807, when the Commissioners allotted to the Overseers of the Poor: –

1. The site of the present school-house and the plots thereto already allotted containing one statute acre.

2. A plot of land containing two statute acres.

3. And another plot of land containing 38 perches, to be for ever held and enjoyed by the Overseers of the Poor of the Township of Sale for the time being, in trust for the inhabitants of the said township to the intent that the rents and profits might be applied for the benefit and support of the said school, according to the ancient constitution thereof.

The fourth acquisition of property consists of a sum of money from the Railway Company which had taken possession of some land belonging to the school and other land belonging to the township. The Overseers received £153.16s.9d. [£153.83½p] as compensation which was invested for the use of the school.

Since the railway was opened an unusual number of dwelling-houses has been yearly erected; the population has rapidly increased and will probably continue to do so for many years to come. One-third of the township at least has within the last ten years been purchased with a view to being shortly built upon. The largest part of the school property is near to the railway station, and is so eligible for building upon, that it may be sold for the highest price given for lands in Sale.'

The pamphlet goes on to say that in November, 1854 a requisition was signed by 47 inhabitants requesting the Overseers to call a meeting of ratepayers with the object of forming a committee to consult with the Overseers on all matters concerning the school. A meeting was convened by public notice and 15 gentlemen were elected as a consulting committee. It was found that the school was very defective with a flagged floor very much out of repair; with one firegrate in a room 33ft. (10.058 metres) by 19ft. 6ins. (5.943 metres). It was cold in winter and the fittings were in bad condition.

The average number of children in attendance for the three years ending 1854 was only 41. The income of the school was about £30 per annum – that it might be increased to £110 per annum or otherwise the property might be sold for at least

£2,200, and for, say, £1,200 a building might be erected, to comprise a master's house and three schoolrooms, one for boys, another for girls and a third for infants, to accommodate 300 scholars, and the remaining £1,000 might be invested to yield an income of £40 p.a. that an improved system of teaching could be introduced, all these advantages without any cost to the inhabitants. So went the findings of the committee.

Application was then made to the Charity Commissioners for permission for this scheme to be put into effect. The scheme also included the appointment of a board of trustees.

There were opponents of the scheme who appear to have been led by the Rev. J. J. Cort, the first incumbent of St. Anne's church, built that year, and the Rev. C. B. Sowerby, the rector. The Rev. J. J. Cort was included on the list of proposed trustees, but Mr. Sowerby was not, although his curate, the Rev. John Hunter, who had been the schoolmaster for 20 years, was included on the list.

Mr. Cort and Mr. Sowerby were also corresponding with the Charity Commissioners, and it was later agreed that Mr. Sowerby be included on the proposed list of trustees.

However, this concession did not satisfy the opposers and it becomes clear, on reading all the correspondence, that they were determined to get a majority of their own supporters on to the board. In a letter to the Commissioners they accuse the Dissenters of attempting to gain control of the management of the school; and further, in a letter to the Commissioners, the Rev. C. B. Sowerby says "We altogether deny the necessity for any change being made in the school, as it is quite equal to meet the wants of that class of scholars who attend it, and for whose benefit it was originally founded".

Although the opposers of the scheme obtained the support of the Charity Commissioners, the Overseers of the Poor stuck to their guns and eventually, after long and protracted correspondence, won their way and the board of trustees was duly recognised by the Charity Commissioners.

Possibly some kind of compromise was agreed upon by the two factions, as the plan envisaged by the consulting committee was not put into effect; the school being gradually improved and extended instead. An infants' school was erected in 1861 and added to in 1874; in 1879 a new school was built on a site now occupied by the National Westminster Bank at the corner of Springfield Road and next to the school which had been erected about 1800.

During the 18th century about 30 schools, excluding grammar schools, were founded in Cheshire. Many of them came under the influence of the Society for Promoting Christian Knowledge; however, the school at Sale does not appear to have done so. In 1812, the Chester Diocesan Society was formed at the desire of the Bishop of Chester. One of the objects of the Society was the making of grants of bibles, prayer books, etc. in the proportion of £6.10s.0d. (£6.50) to every hundred children to every **school in the Diocese in union with the Chester Diocesan School. A number of grants** were made during the first five years, including one to the school at Sale.

It is known which subjects were taught at the township school during the 18th century from the following advertisement which appeared in the Manchester Mercury in 1774.

'WANTED A SCHOOLMASTER for the School at SALE, near Altrincham, in Cheshire, to teach Reading, Writing, and Accounts, Any Person, properly qualified, by applying to the Overseers and Church-wardens of Sale aforesaid will be treated with, and all suitable Encouragement given.'

In 1810 a meeting was called under the chairmanship of Charles White, at which the new school was invested in trustees elected at the meeting, namely, the rector and churchwardens of the parish and twelve other people.

Mr. Heap was elected schoolmaster. Later, it was decided to provide a "proper residence" for Mr. Heap and this was accomplished by the simple procedure of the Overseers of the Poor giving immediate notice to Joseph Royle and Widow Williamson to quit the premises called the Old School, which had been converted to poorhouses.

Mr. Heap remained as schoolmaster and town secretary until 1818, and at the township meeting of May 23 of that year it was agreed that "the Overseers of the Poor of Sale should immediately advertise for Candidates for a Schoolmaster" and also that "a few Hand Bills shall be printed and distributed at the Discretion of the Overseers . . .".

At a meeting of June 29, 1818, called to elect the new schoolmaster, it was decided that "it was absolutely necessary for a candidate to understand the theory and practice of Mensuration, have a good hand and read correctly". Mr. William Sadler was elected as schoolmaster for one year to commence midsummer, 1818.

However, the following November, it was decided to again advertise for a new schoolmaster and, on December 28, 1818 the Rev. J. Hunter was elected to the post. Mr. Sadler then refused to give up possession of the house and in fact did not do so until the following May.

Mr. Hunter was the schoolmaster until 1836, when he resigned and James Warren was elected in his place. He paid a token quarterly rent of 1/- (5p) for the "school, schoolhouse and premises" and "enjoyed" to act as secretary for the town, and to "make out all ley-books and books of assessment" for the Overseers and other officers, and "to prepare the accounts of the provident society previous to the distribution of the fund at Christmas".

It was decided that "if at any future time the Landowners of Sale should be desirous to have a Schoolmistress to teach Knitting and Sewing . . . Mr. Warren agrees to provide a proper Person . . .". It was agreed at the same time that Mr. Warren's "Holy days [were] to be a fortnight at Christmas and Midsummer the whole of Saturdays the hours of teaching from eight o'clock to twelve in the morning and from half-past One to half-past four in the Evening".

In 1831 the population of Sale had reached 1,104 and in Ashton, 974, where a private school had appeared, being attended, in 1833, by 14 boys and 38 girls at the expense of their parents. Two private schools also existed in Sale attended in total by 26 boys and 28 girls, also at their parents' expense. In addition there was a Sunday School at Ashton attended by 49 boys and 56 girls; this was supported by annual collections, as were four Sunday Schools in Sale belonging, respectively, to the Independents (Congregationalists), attendance 140 children; Unitarians, attendance 15; one which commenced in 1820 belonging to the Wesleyan Methodists, attendance 104; each of these three having a lending library and, lastly, one belonging to the Primitive Methodists which commenced in 1824 and was attended by 73 children.

The township school, in 1833, was attended by 42 boys and eight girls and was partly supported by a small payment from each child which by 1840 was, annually, 3/- (15p) for reading, 6/- (30p) for reading and writing and 8/- (40p) for reading, writing and arithmetic. In 1870 education was made compulsory, but fees had to be paid; parents who were too poor to pay had to apply to the Poor Law Guardians. In 1872, education became compulsory and free.

The influx of middle-class people into Sale from Manchester and elsewhere started after the railway opened in 1849, many of them were Dissenters who would not agree to public money being spent on education under the influence of the Church of England.

The British and Foreign School Society under Dissenting patronage worked on the basis of undenominational Bible teaching. The Church of England countered with the National Society for the Education of the Poor according to the Principles of the Church of England. Therefore, in the 19th century most schools were either "British" or, in the case of villages, usually "National".

Sale township school had, by 1860, become a British school and the attendance was about 150. It was probably due to the Dissenters having obviously taken control of the township school that St. Anne's C. of E. School was erected in 1863, the parish of St. Anne having been formed seven years earlier.

The plot of land for the school was sold in 1862 by Samuel Brooks to the "Incumbent and Churchwardens of Sale for the purpose of a school", the price of the half-acre of land was £166.7s.6d. (£166.37½p). The school was to be for "the education of children and adults or children only of the labouring manufacturing and other poorer classes" and it was to be a National School.

A committee of management was set up consisting of the Minister, curate, the churchwardens and ten others, namely; William Butterfield, merchant; Alfred Milne, Esq.; James Pendlebury, cashier; John Livesy, merchant; John King, merchant; Alfred Watkin, merchant; William Wilson, architect; John Arnold, grocer; Samuel Swire, coal proprietor and Robert Marsland, cotton spinner and "such other person(s) continuing to be contributors in every year to the amount of Twenty shillings each at the least to the funds of the said School and to be members of the Church of England . . .". No person was to be appointed a teacher who was not a member of the Church of England.

In 1839 the Primitive Methodists built a school–chapel on Northenden Road where the present chapel stands. The next school–chapel to be erected in Sale was St. Joseph's R.C. in 1866; by the time it closed, at the end of the century, the attendance was over 100. The school–chapel was replaced by the present school in 1899 at a cost of £2,000.

Other church schools built during the 19th century were St. Martin's Parochial School, the foundation stone for which was laid in 1874 and St. Mary Magdalene Higher Grade, opened in 1896. Among secular schools opened in the 19th century in Sale was Sale Lodge School, built in 1854 by Edmund Howarth who lived at Sale Lodge, now the Golf Clubhouse. This school was situated at the junction of Fairy Lane and Wythenshawe Road near a pond and was known locally as the marl pit school. In 1876 the Manchester Certified Industrial School for Girls was built in Northenden Road, just inside the Sale boundary, to accommodate 100 girls and was certified April 21, 1877.

During the 18th and early 19th centuries there was a proliferation of private schools in England, many of them short-lived. The earliest example that I know of in Sale was in Cross Street. An advertisement was placed in the Manchester Mercury in 1769 which read:–

'AT a commodious House, pleasantly situated in a healthy Air, in Cross-street, near Altringham, in Cheshire. Girls boarded and instructed in all sorts of Needlework, Spelling, Reading, Writing, and Accompts, by

SAMUEL and CATHARINE SCHOLES.

N.B.   The Price for Board is only Ten Guineas per Annum, Schooling included Gentlemen or Ladies may likewise Board on Reasonable Terms.'

The "commodious house" referred to was probably the late 17th century building which stood almost opposite Mersey Road and is called the "tree-embowered Manor House" in Mrs. Linnaeus Banks's "The Manchester Man" but by 1901 a directory names it less grandly as the Old Manor House Laundry. It was more recently the premises of Magnet Joinery until its demolition about 1982.

The first church was, of course, St. Martin's parish church; the list of rectors was traced back to 1305 by the late Raymond Richards, although the foundation of the church may be older. It is said there is a tradition that the church is built on the site of a chantry or cell of the Virgin Mary, but there is no known evidence to support this. The present building dates from 1714; the baptistry being added in 1874 and the tower and lychgate in 1887.

During the Civil War and the Interregnum, the parish church had two Presbyterian rectors. This was probably due to the influence of Sir William Brereton of

Handforth, the patron of the living, as Brereton was an uncompromising Puritan; although during this period the incumbents were, supposedly, "freely selected" by the parishioners.

John Ford was the second and last of the two Presbyterian rectors, his death occuring in 1661. After this time the Presbyterians probably met in the house of one of their number until a chapel was built; the chapel is first mentioned in 1716. It stood on the north side of Glebelands Road, at its junction with Cross Street and it had a burial ground.

In 1743–4 a new chapel was built in Chapel Road and the old one was demolished, its materials being used for building purposes, the gravestones being used to flag the yards of houses in Cross Street. The building in Chapel Road survived until 1972 when it was demolished.

The second half of the 18th century saw the chapel gradually turning to Unitarianism; the baptismal register for this period showed the names of parents who lived in Stretford, Partington, Baguley, Cross Bank and Sinderland. In 1876 a new chapel, now demolished, was built in Atkinson Road.

The Wesleyan Methodists had organised meetings in Sale as early as 1773, but their first chapel was not built until 1820, on a site now occupied by No. 123 Broad Road. A further chapel on the site of the present Town Hall was bought from the Congregationalists and used from 1853, being replaced by the Wesley Chapel in School Road in 1860 on a site now occupied by Boots, a new building being erected in The Avenue in 1963. Meanwhile, Broad Road Chapel was superseded, in 1875, by Trinity Methodist Chapel in Northenden Road and the Primitive Methodists, in 1872–3, had replaced their school–chapel with a new one.

The Congregationalists began cottage services in Sale about 1800. It is possible that seceders from the Presbyterian chapel, which had turned to Unitarianism, formed the bulk of the congregation. Early in the 19th century they had a chapel at Sale Bridge which they later sold to the Methodists after opening a larger chapel in Montague Road in 1852. The Sale Bridge chapel became the Institute, a sort of public hall, after 1860 and was latterly the home of the firm of Fowler's Calculators until it was demolished to make room for the Town Hall. In 1893, the Congregationalists built a chapel in Ashton on a site at the corner of Park Avenue and Cross Street.

The Baptists also built their chapel in Ashton, in 1875, at Ashton Lane on a site not far from the Meeting House of the Society of Friends which had been erected in Park Road in 1856. The Presbyterians returned to Sale in 1874, in the form of the Scottish Presbyterian church, having built their chapel in Northenden Road. The church of St. Mary Magdalene at the corner of Moss Lane and Harboro Road was also completed in 1874. St. Paul's Church was built in Springfield Road in 1883 for the purpose of forming a new parish in Sale and, the following year, the Parish of St. Paul came into being as St. Anne's Parish, formed in 1856, was under pressure due to the increasing population; the church had been built in 1854.

Plate 15: The Meeting House of the Society of Friends, Park Road, erected in 1856. In 1673 the Manchester Friends acquired a plot of ground in Deansgate which they used as a burial ground until 1847. During 1876-7, the remains were disinterred and deposited in a vault in the burial ground in Park Road.

It has been generally supposed that the first Roman Catholics in Sale after the Reformation were 19th century Irish immigrants, the idea being strengthened by the Rector's statement in the Bishop's Visitation of 1778, when he said "There are not any Papists in the Parish". There was, however, in the late 17th or early 18th centuries, a Catholic family in Sale named Chadwick and, as late as the 19th century, there was a field called Chadwick's Meadow. In 1745 John Chadwick, described as a yeoman of Sale, leased a forge in Charnock Richard, and it was probably then that the family left Sale. About 1870 St. Joseph's school–chapel was extended and, in 1885, it was replaced by the present church on an adjoining site in Hope Road.

The number of churches built in Sale and elsewhere during the 19th century is quite remarkable and they were usually well-attended. It is unavoidable to contrast this with the present day. It can also be contrasted with the preceeding century; in

1778 the Rector of the parish, Richard Popplewell Johnson, stated "We have prayers and a sermon likewise upon Good Friday and Christmas Day, but seldom on other Holidays, as few or none attend".

Sources for Chapter 7 – Education and Religion

Cornwall–Legh Muniments.

An Address to the Rate payers and Inhabitants of Sale by the Overseers of the Poor, 1856.

History and Gazetteer of Cheshire. Francis White and co. 1860.

The Cheshire Sheaf. September, 1954, p. 43.

Powicke, Fred, James. Centenary History of the Cheshire Congregational Union (1806–1906), 1907.

Urwick, William. Nonconformity in Cheshire, 1864.

Manchester Mercury. February 21, 1769; April 5, 1774.

Sale Township Minutes.

Abstract of Education Returns, 1833.

Census returns, 1831.

Deeds and papers of the Brooks family.

Sale Tithe Award, 1844.

Ashton-on-Mersey Tithe Award, 1845.

Slater's Directories, 1899–1910.

The Charities in the County of Chester, 1840.

Awty, B. G. Charcoal Ironmasters of Cheshire and Lancashire 1600–1785.

Transactions Historic Society of Lancashire and Cheshire, vol. 109, 1957.

Bishop's Visitation Book, 1778.

This sculpted head, of millstone-grit, was found on the site when the Lindow Tavern, Sale, was rebuilt during the 1960s. This recent photograph was sent to Martin Petch at the Manchester Museum. Mr. Petch, who has made a special study of stone heads found in the region, states that *"it appears to be a Medieval or possibly post-Medieval corbel, presumably ecclesiastical in nature and from a church ..."*

A corbel is a projecting member of stone or timber built into a wall to carry a load such as a roof truss; the head has been fashioned so that it gazes in a downward direction. There is a remote possibility that it originated in our old parish church of St. Martin which was rebuilt in 1714.

8

The Post Office
and the Railway

A Master of the Posts was appointed in England as long ago as the reign of Henry VIII and a postal service organised connecting London with certain other places along the more important roads, the letters being carried by post-horse. The nearest post-road to this area, however, came up from London through Coventry, proceeding westwards to Lichfield, Stone, Nantwich and Chester and then to "Rudland" and along the North Wales coast to Anglesey. There was probably no post-road to Manchester before the 17th century. At that time the post-road to Manchester and London was the Holyhead or Chester road for most of the way, through St. Albans, Towcester, Daventry, Coventry, Lichfield, Stone and Knutsford, after which it joined what is now the A56 through Sale and over Crossford Bridge.

After 1750, certain highways began to be properly surfaced, making it possible for the mail-coach service to begin and the summer of 1785 saw the first mail-coach service to Manchester. The routes were gradually increased until they covered a wide network of roads. There were, eventually, services from Manchester to Liverpool and Chester but the mail-coaches went via Warrington and, therefore, did not pass through Sale and Altrincham. Instead, some mail was carried along this route by post-coaches which were stage-coaches contracting to carry mail. The guard on the mail-coach was armed with a blunderbuss which, at close range, was a terribly destructive weapon; although the robbing of stage-coaches was not uncommon there is not a single example of a mail-coach being robbed.

By the middle of the 19th century the mail-coach had given way to the railway; however, in 1894, a horse-drawn mail-coach was again introduced to carry the mail between Manchester and Liverpool, the railway being discarded for this purpose. The guard and driver were armed with revolvers and continued to be until the coaches were replaced by motor vehicles in 1902.

The end of the 18th century saw the spread of local penny posts. The Manchester penny post began in April, 1793 with the announcement that letters would be received at the principal office in Back Square and four other places, that deliveries would be made "all over the town at 8, 12.30 and 6" and that letter-carriers would take penny-post letters six days a week to Middleton. Ashton-under-Lyne, Stalybridge, Oldham and Saddleworth "and other places of which due notice will be given". The 'other places' by 1835 included over 30 villages outside Manchester.

It is quite likely that the post from Manchester to Sale was carried with the Altrincham and Knutsford post in the late 18th century and delivered to a receiving office on Cross Street. This Manchester–Knutsford service was discontinued by 1801 due to the establishment of a mail-coach service from Manchester directly to Birmingham and, in the resulting controversy involving the Earl of Stamford, which lasted for many years, a report referring to the Altrincham route indicates Hulme, Cornbrook, Hullart (sic), Old Trafford and Cross Street.

The post for Ashton and Sale was later delivered on foot from Stretford. Henry Moore, son and successor of James Moore who kept Stretford Post Office early in the 19th century, died in 1900 aged 84. He stated that until June, 1835, the mail was made up and received on alternate days. The mail-coach plied between Manchester and Knutsford and, as a boy, he had to rise early and collect the Stretford mail from the coach as it made a brief halt there. The delivery of letters was at first only made along the main road. Gradually the service was extended "across the river by Jackson's Boat into Cheshire to Sale Moor, crossing the main road at Pillocan [Pelican] Brook to Ashton-on-Mersey . . .".

The local post from Manchester was delivered on horseback. A directory of 1825 states "From Manchester letters are despatched by County Messenger attached to the Two-Penny Post Office to . . . Stretford, Cross-Street, Ashton-upon-Mersey, &c. on Mon. Wed. and Fri . . . .". Also listed are the post-coaches to Chester, Shrewsbury and Nantwich, which called at Altrincham.

There was a Post Office at Sale in 1858 and possibly before then, the postmaster was Samuel Brindley; letters from all parts were delivered there from Manchester each morning and afternoon and letters sent to Manchester from all parts shortly after mid-day and in the evening. Later, the Post Office was taken over by George Birkenhead, a shoemaker born in Great Budworth, his shop where the postal service was conducted was on Washway Road, almost opposite to where the former Pyramid cinema stands. In 1860, the letters arrived at the Post Office at 6.00 a.m. and 4.40 p.m. and were despatched at 12.15 and 8.20 p.m.

There was also a Post Office receiving box at Sale Moor, as the area around the Legh Arms had become known as by the second half of the 19th century, this was at Thomas Wilkinson's shop, Moor Lane, or 170 Northenden Road as it later became.

The electric telegraph arrived early in the 19th century and various people were responsible for its development. As long ago as 1819 a Dane, Hans Christian Oersted, discovered by accident that a wire carrying an electric current would deflect a magnetic needle. In 1835 the American, Samuel Morse, constructed an instrument in which a tapping key switched an electric current on and off working an electromagnet which caused a pencil to mark a moving strip of paper; he then developed his code to use with it.

In the meantime two Englishmen, Charles Wheatstone and William Cooke, were carrying out experiments with a telegraph system and, in 1839, the world's first telegraph system was built between Paddington and West Drayton. After this the use of the telegraph spread rapidly, Charles Wheatstone devising the forerunner of the modern punched tape system. In 1870, the private companies were taken over by the Post Office, involving the transfer of 2,800 telegraph offices. Apart from sending normal messages the telegraph also transmitted news from the early editions of the London papers to the newsrooms in most of the large towns. The telegraph wires were carried between the towns by the railways which developed more or less contemporaneously with the electric telegraph.

The 1871 census shows that two of George Birkenhead's daughters were employed as telegraphists at Sale and one of his three sons was a telegraph messenger; at the same time his wife was the postmistress. George Birkenhead's youngest son, Albert, eventually became the postmaster (probably about 1883) and, by the last decade of the 19th century, 170 Northenden Road was a sub-Post Office handling money orders and a savings bank with John Wood as sub-postmaster with a further sub-Post Office at 141 Marsland Road where the sub-postmaster was Walter Vaughan.

By the beginning of the 20th century a purpose-built Post Office had been erected next to Birkenhead's shop and it was now described as a post, money order and telegraph office, savings bank and Annuity and Insurance Office. The staff included, as well as the postmaster, four clerks, five telegraph messengers and 23 postmen, dealing with 66,000 letters and 1,200 parcels a week.

There were also sub-Post Offices at Green Lane and Cross Street, Ashton. A few years later the sub-Post Office at Sale Moor was moved to 162 Northenden Road and expanded to be a telegraph office, savings bank and Insurance Office. In the early years of the 20th century the postal service reached its peak of efficiency with frequent deliveries of letters. From the head Post Office on Washway Road on week-days, four deliveries a day were made, at 7.00 a.m., 12.00 noon, 3.00 p.m. and 6.00 p.m.; the telegraph service functioned twelve hours a day from 8.00 a.m. to 8.00 p.m. The Post Office was open for stamps, postal orders, etc. from 7.00 a.m. to 9.00 p.m. and until 8.00 p.m. for money orders and the savings bank. On Sunday there was one delivery of letters at 7.00 a.m. and the telegraph operated from 8.00 a.m. until 10.00 a.m.

In 1924, the Manchester postal authorities and the Corporation Tramways Committee entered into a very useful arrangement. By the running of "post-cars" residents in the principal suburbs were able to post their evening mail later than the normal suburban collections and ensure delivery by the first morning post. During the first four weeks of the new system 8,000 letters were dealt with, the number increasing gradually to 17,000 by the end of March that year. Fourteen routes were covered by the post-cars, each tramcar leaving its suburban terminus in time to arrive in the city at

Plate 16: Sale's first purpose-built Post Office which ceased to be used as such when the present Post Office was opened in 1931. The Post Office sign on the gable is still faintly discernible.

9.30p.m. The tram which carried the post from Altrincham left at 8.26p.m. and another left Sale Moor at 8.46p.m. The tramcars were normal service vehicles and mail could be posted at any stop along the route; they were distinguished by the words "Post Car" above the route number and operated each night from Monday to Friday.

The proposal to build the present Post Office on Washway Road was first announced in 1927. This was followed by a letter from Sale and Ashton Traders' Association to the Postmaster at Manchester which stated that it was understood that a new Post Office and automatic telephone exchange was to be built in Sale. The traders objected to the location of the proposed site and suggested an alternative site in School Road at the corner of Claremont Road. The uncharitable among us may have suspected that, as most of the traders would be located in School Road, their motive was based on the hope that the new Post Office would attract business their way; such was not the case, their motives were entirely altruistic, being compounded of a mixture of concern for civic pride and the safety of the public.

The traders pointed out that although this was to be Sale's new Post Office, if it was built on the north-west side of Washway Road then it would be in Ashton. Also, the Sale people would have to cross a busy main road in order to reach it. In their anxiety to protect the public from danger the traders overlooked the fact that should the Post Office be built in School Road then Ashton people would have to cross the main road. However, this was pointed out to them in a subsequent reply by the Postmaster General in the House of Commons where he dismissed the objections in spite of Sale Council supporting the traders' views and their case being put by A. E. Townsend, M.P. for Stockport. The Post Office and telephone exchange was built on the site where it still stands, and opened for postal transactions on Sunday, September 20, 1931; the manual exchange in the old Post Office remaining in operation for some months afterwards.

By 1934, with a total staff of 56 including 43 postmen, the number of deliveries of post daily had fallen from four at the beginning of the century to three, with 80,000 letters and 1,300 parcels a week being delivered. By this date there were 1,941 telephone subscribers in Sale and Ashton.

The inventor of the telephone is recognised as being Alexander Graham Bell, an Edinburgh man who emigrated to North America at the age of 23 and first transmitted speech in Boston in 1876. In 1878, Bell demonstrated his telephone over here and, in 1879, The Telephone Company was formed, opening the first telephone exchange in the U.K. in London. Later that year another exchange was opened in London by the Edison Telephone Company using an instrument working on a quite different principle to that of Bell's and invented by Thomas Alva Edison, an American. In 1880 the two companies amalgamated under the name of the United Telephone Company.

Manchester had a telephone service right at the beginning, the Edison Telephone Company having opened premises in Cross Street, Manchester. A rival firm, The Lancashire Telephonic Exchange Company, brought into service the first manually operated telephone exchange in the north-west at Manchester in 1879; this was in Faulkner Street. The United Telephone Company and the Lancashire Telephonic combined in 1881 to form the Lancashire and Cheshire Telephonic Exchange Co. Ltd. with the head office at 38 Faulkner Street.

This company created quite a comprehensive telephone service in Manchester in its early days; as well as the normal telephone service between subscribers who paid a tariff of £20 a year, the company would install private lines between several branches of a firm as well as internal telephones in hotels, factories, etc. There was a telegram-phone service in Manchester, Liverpool and Blackburn and public call-stations were set up. In addition to this the company would install electric bells and fire and burglar alarms.

The telephone lines from Manchester served many intermediate places between Manchester and Liverpool. In 1886 lines were in course of construction by the Lancashire and Cheshire Company through Stretford to Sale, Altrincham and Bowdon; and to Ashton-on-Mersey, Carrington, etc., to Warburton. By November, 1888 these lines were in operation. The following year the Lancashire and Cheshire Company was absorbed into the National Telephone Company and within a few years tariffs were reduced to £6 a year. Early in 1912 the G.P.O. took over all the local telephone services with the exception of Hull and Guernsey.

Mention has been made of stage and mail-coaches in the 18th and early 19th centuries; a previous chapter dealt briefly with the Bridgewater Canal and reference has been made to the deplorable condition of the main road through Sale, typical of the state of many of the roads in England at this period so that, although a long-distance haulage firm like Pickfords began operating in the 18th century, movement of goods and passengers by road was painfully slow and only marginally quicker by canal. By road, local carriers using horse-drawn wagons ran regular services from Manchester, through Sale, to Altrincham.

Until 1849 road and water transport were the only choices that people in Sale had, both to move goods and to travel. Quite early in the 19th century a horse-bus service began operating from the Commercial Inn, Brown Street, Manchester with four buses a day to Altrincham and Dunham. Another service ran a vehicle every hour from St. Ann Street, Manchester to Altrincham in 1845 and, by 1864, three buses each day ran from Manchester to "Sale Moor Pitts".

The railway era, which got under way in the 1830s, gave the impetus to the Industrial Revolution which it needed. It not only revolutionised transport to the extent that roads were now seldom used for travelling long distances; but also the construction of the railways created a demand for engineering skills on a large scale, with the widespread use of templates and gauges for the manufacture of standard parts. Manchester became the centre of the world's engineering industry; by 1851, agriculture was no longer predominant and the urban and rural populations were about equal.

The social consequences were far-reaching; the towns now being governed by a totally different type of person – the new middle-class, many of them although wealthy only one or two generations removed from the working-class. The railways enabled the middle-class to move away from the manufacturing towns and have country homes built, usually within a short distance of a railway station. The wealthier of them in the Manchester area bought land and had "villas" built in places like Wilmslow and Bowdon to the disgust of their hereditary landowning neighbours who referred to them as "Cottontots" – a reference to the source of the wealth of most of the newcomers.

The dispute concerning the township school in Sale, dealt with in the previous chapter, showed that in Sale, also, the old landowners' influence was now in decline as the smaller merchants, entrepreneurs and professional people began to move into the area. The new wealth being generated nationally, vastly improved the wages of the working-class in the manufacturing towns, and inevitably, affected the wages of the rural population in places like Sale, close to manufacturing towns.

On July 25, 1845, The Manchester South Junction and Altrincham Railway Act was passed; the capital being subscribed by the Manchester and Birmingham Railway Company and the Sheffield and Manchester Railway Company. This Act was the beginning of a process which was to change Sale more profoundly in two or three decades than anything which had happened in the preceding two or three centuries.

The railway consisted of two parts, the first, the South Junction line, connecting the lines at London Road station with the London and North-Western Railway at Ordsall Lane, Salford; and the second, the Manchester and Altrincham line, about eight miles in length; the railway being opened for passenger and goods traffic on July 21, 1849. The contractor for the Manchester–Altrincham section was John Brogden of Sale.

At the Sale township meeting held on January 2, 1845, it was "unanimously resolved that as the proposed line of Railway from Manchester to Birkenhead will be very prejudicial and injurious to Property, Roads and Public Highways within this Township generally, we the undersigned do agree to dissent from the said proposed line so far as we are concerned in the said undertaking". A list of eight names follows the resolution. John Brogden's name is to be found among the list; he had not previously attended a township meeting for almost four years.

The first train from Manchester on the opening day started at 8.00 a.m. as did the first train from Altrincham which, after some delay at Stretford, reached Oxford Road station within an hour carrying 65 passengers. The next train left Altrincham at 8.40 a.m. and was the express, consisting solely of first-class passengers. It carried 15 passengers and completed the journey in 18 minutes. The regular service consisted of 13 trains each way, one about every hour from 8.00 a.m. to 9.00 p.m. except Saturday when the last train left Manchester at 10.00 p.m. and Altrincham at 9.30 p.m. On Sundays there were nine trains from Manchester and eight from Altrincham. All

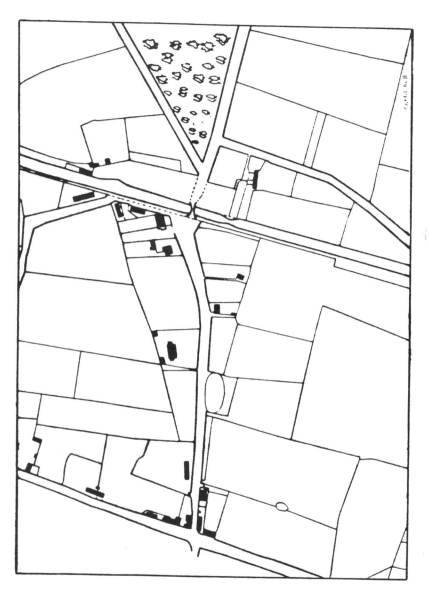

Fig. 4: The map shown above is based on the 1844 Tithe Map and the map opposite is part of the 1876 Ordnance Survey, both showing the area which is now Sale town centre, with School Road and part of Northenden Road running from left to right and crossing the canal, the increase in building density from 1844-76 is clearly shown. The plantation shown on the right of the 1844 map still partly existed by 1876 and is inside the triangle formed by Northenden Road, Broad Road and Woodlands Road

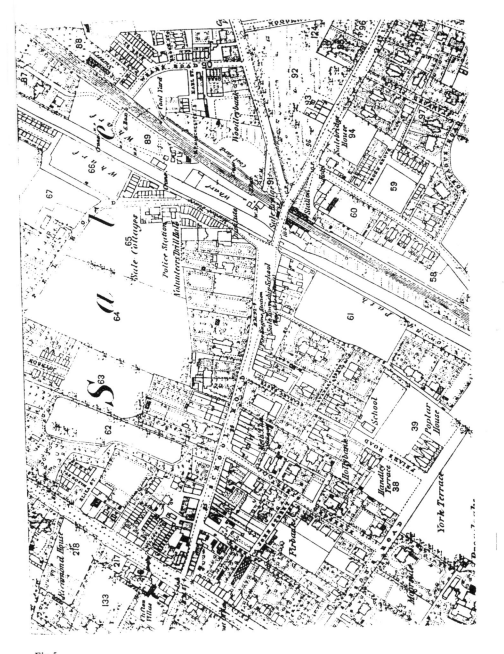

Fig 5

the trains except the express carried 1st, 2nd and 3rd class passengers. The express took 20 minutes for the journey and the ordinary train half-an-hour.

The fare on the express was 1/- (5p); other trains, first-class 10d. (4p), second-class 8d. (3½p), third-class 6d. (2½p), with a proportionate charge for intermediate stations; the stations being Oxford Road, Old Trafford, Stretford, Sale, Timperley and Altrincham. Later an extension was made to the foot of the Downs, the new terminus being known as Bowdon Station.

A few weeks before the opening of the line the contractors made an experimental trip along the Altrincham section and invited a number of friends. Amongst the party were Alexander and John Brogden. Attached to the engine was a covered carriage in which was stationed the Stretford Temperance Band and two first-class carriages loaned by the Manchester and Liverpool Railway to carry the party which met at noon.

Plate 17: *Flora,* built in 1849, one of the early locomotives which operated on the Manchester, South Junction and Altrincham Railway.

The train started amidst cheers from the railway workers and others assembled at the starting point. At Stretford a crowd had gathered to welcome the train and the band played. At Sale employees of Brogden turned out and cheered amidst the firing of cannon and other demonstrations of welcome; similarly at Timperley. At Altrincham the excursionists, headed by the band, marched to the Unicorn Hotel.

Some modifications were made during construction; apparently a badly designed bridge at Manchester which could have been strengthened was scrapped at a cost of £1,200 and working out an improved design caused delay. At Altrincham an elaborate station was started, the cost being disproportionate to the needs of the traffic; it was arranged to suspend the work while a plan was prepared for a light timber building, avoiding the massive arches and pillars in the original design.

Sale station, or Sale Moor as it was called until 1856, was also originally built from timber, the present building being erected during the 1870s. Altrincham and Bowdon stations were closed when a new station named "Altrincham and Bowdon" was opened in 1881. Brooklands station was not built until 1859, ten years after the railway opened, and it was not until July, 1931, two months after electrification, that Dane Road station came into use.

The Manchester South Junction and Altrincham Railway was electrified at an estimated cost of half a million pounds and powered by D.C. current. This system lasted for forty years until May, 1971, when the present 25,000 volts A.C. system was introduced.

Sources for Chapter 8 – The Post Office and the Railway

Aston, Joseph. Picture of Manchester. 1816.

Transactions Lancashire and Cheshire Antiquarian Society, vol. 22, 1904.

Baines, Edward. History, Directory and Gazetteer of the County Palatine of Lancaster, 1825.

Sale and Stretford Guardian Year Book, 1904.

Free Lance magazine, vol. 3, 1868, p. 399.

Postal Service. Box 242, Manchester Central Library.

Slater's Directory of Manchester, 1887, facing pp. 261; 263.

Town Clerk's Cuttings Book, 1926–9, pp. 24; 41.

The Municipal Journal, vol. 33, May 2, 1924, p. 496.

Sale and Ashton-on-Mersey Year Book, 1925; 1926.

History and Gazetteer of Cheshire. Francis White and Co. 1860.

Sale Year Book, 1903.

Census returns, 1871.

Slater's Directory of Manchester and Liverpool, 1858.

Slater's Directory of Manchester, 1845.

Pigot's Directory of Manchester, 1841.

Kelly's Directory of Cheshire, 1864.

The Manchester South Junction and Altrincham Railway, 1899.

Henry Booth, Inventor, 1980.

Sale Charter Inquiry Evidence, 1934.

The Builder, July 31, 1875.

Sale and Stretford Guardian, September 18, 1931.

9

The Creation of Urban Sale

The opening of the railway immensely increased the value of much of the land which had comprised the former common, Sale Moor. This land, it will be remembered, had remained waste until the Napoleonic Wars created an increased demand at home for food; consequently, a great deal of poor-quality land was brought into cultivation for the first time, and it was precisely because the soil of the common was not very productive that Sale Moor, reaching roughly from the main road in the west to the Legh Arms, had remained a common until 1807. The soil in that area is still thin today as the Parks Department know in their experience of cultivating both Worthington Park and Walkden Gardens.

However, after 1849, that part of the former common within reasonable distance of the railway station suddenly changed from being the least valuable land in Sale to the most highly-priced for the purpose of erecting houses. One of the first houses in Sale to be built for what was to be a steady influx of the Manchester merchant and professional classes into the area was Vernon Lodge (now Brooklands Lodge guesthouse) Marsland Road, in 1851. This house was built for Peter Royle, a Manchester-born surgeon, and his wife, Mariann, as the monogrammed datestone on the gable-end testifies; but the process did not really get under way until the 1860s when "villas" were springing up both on Sale Moor and, to a lesser extent Ashton-on-Mersey, in the Ashton Lane and Harboro Road area.

Most of the houses still exist and, with few exceptions, are quite modest compared to those built in Bowdon for the wealthier merchants. Whatever the size of the house the materials used by the Victorian builders were always sound and only well-seasoned timber was used. The houses reflected the standing of the people who occupied them and contemporary architectural drawings refer to 1st to 5th-class houses. Towards the end of the 19th century, the housing demands of the middle-class in Sale having been largely met, smaller, semi-detached houses were built for the growing managerial class and yet smaller ones for artisans and the increasing army of clerks; these latter houses were either semi-detached or in terraces, often distinguished by a name and, whenever possible, the house-numbers were not used, this practice persisting until the 1930s. These small and middle-sized houses were almost always rented.

Plate 18: This house on Marsland Road, *Vernon Lodge* (now Brooklands Lodge guest house), was built in 1851 for Peter Royle, a Manchester surgeon, and his wife Marrian. It is probably the first urban house to be built in Sale; that is, a house with no agricultural connection, built after the opening of the railway.

The house is an enigma; it cannot be described as polite and is certainly not vernacular. It is so unusual with its first-floor entrance that I sought the opinion of John H.G. Archer of Manchester University School of Architecture who agrees that the house is "unusual to the point of eccentricity both in general detail and in the treatment of the entrance....Altogether it is an oddity; partly handsome....and certainly designed to impress".

When the house was built an uninterrupted view of rural tranquillity in Sale and Baguley would be obtained from the first-floor apartments, which may be one reason for Peter Royle's choice of such an extraordinary but charming design.

At about the same time, terraces of workers' "cottages" were erected for rent, often without a garden and usually occupied by the unskilled. Again, these houses were also mainly built on the former common in Sale, the indigenous farm-workers continuing to live largely in the cottages erected before the time of the railway and situated for the most part in the traditional farming areas.

For example, a row of terrace houses, built about 1873 in Perseverance Street, was occupied in 1881 by sixteen heads of families of whom only four were born in Sale; one of these, a market gardener, was named Leigh and two others, farm labourers, named Marsland and Gratrix. The rest of the heads of families comprising four gardeners, a painter, joiner, house carpenter, porter, plasterer, bootmaker and a nurse were born variously in Manchester, Crewe, Siddington, Chorlton-cum-Hardy, Cumberland, Hereford and Bermondsey. During the 1930s, Perseverance Street was absorbed into Conway Road; only two of the original houses now remain, the rest being demolished some years ago and a block of flats built on the site.

The first chapter noted that the Early English were colonisers rather than immigrants; the opening of the railway started a rather similar process in miniature in Sale. For the middle-class of Manchester who settled here eventually dominated and transformed the place socially and economically. Many of them, although their businesses were located in Manchester and adjacent towns were not by origin Lancastrians; the census returns show that their places of birth ranged from Scotland, through the midlands, to the southern counties of England. As we have seen, by 1874 there were enough Scottish Presbyterians in the area to warrant a church being built in Northenden Road. Similarly their domestic servants; very few of them were local, their places of birth were just as varied.

Before the urbanisation of Sale, the roads which had been laid out on the enclosed common were not properly named; in 1812, these roads were measured and entered in the township minute book above the signature J. Heap. Mr. Heap was the town secretary and schoolmaster, and it is not difficult to imagine him taking a party of his pupils out for a practical exercise in measurement and calculation. A typical example is what was later to be Irlam Road, identified in 1812 as "From Northen Road to Broad Lane nr. Clark's Hey". Naturally, when the sophisticated middle-class began to occupy the former common, such an unwieldy address was unsuitable, and so the roads began to be properly named.

An entry in the township minutes of March 19, 1857, pointed to the gradual urbanisation of Sale, when the Surveyors of Highways were "empowered and are instructed to erect at the termini of the various Streets and Lanes . . . Direction Posts and that the names of the said Streets and Lanes be affixed thereto"; but the newcomers were not willing to live in "lanes" and, by 1866, Wardle Lane changed to Wardle Road, with most of the other lanes on Sale Moor similarly changing before 1870.

The variety of accents to be heard in Sale for a few decades after, say, 1860 must have been quite remarkable and one wonders what the indigenous tenant farmer and labourer bearing a name like Renshaw, Gresty, Marsland or Gratrix, his roots in Sale often going back centuries, must have made of all this. Enormous changes were taking place, wrought by these prosperous strangers, in what had seemed to him to be a fairly permanent way of life; changes which he was powerless to prevent even had he wished to do so.

The nearest that we can get to a contemporary description of this influx to Sale about 120 years ago is the following account from a magazine of 1868 with its rather laboured humour:

'A walk from the station to the slightly mysterious region Cross Street would convey an impression that nothing could be wanting, to those prepared to pay for their supplies. The initiated know that those establishments which are not engaged in the sale of articles absolutely necessary for a bare subsistence are little better than useless. When other things are inquired for, it invariably happens that "we are just out of those" or "expecting them in the day after tomorrow". Of course, it is possible to harden oneself to that sort of thing. Indeed, we believe some ladies who are enthusiasts in the fine art of shopping have learnt to enjoy it. But till such happy state of mind is attained, the habit is not unlikely to lead to displays of wrath. Some few other drawbacks there are in the social station of Sale for which art and not nature are chiefly responsible. Of these not the least palpable is the scarcity of lamps. With the exception of some three or four in Brooklands, no artificial lights have been considered necessary. On winter nights which happen to be moonless and starless, Sale is the most woefully dark place imaginable. The sight of nervous old ladies poking their way about, with the assistance of little hand lanterns, should be sufficient not merely to touch the hearts of the least tender of Local Boards, but even to spur the authorities to action of some sort.

It is not possible to describe the general aspect of the district as either cheerful or enlivening . . . the streets or roads are long dreary stretches of macadam and parapet, adorned with an elaborate system of finger posts, giving the name of the road and the exact number of yards to the station. The whole neighbourhood is barren and monotonously flat. Its flatness is so extreme that, compared with it, the level of the proverbial pancake approaches quite an Alpine character. If an eminence as mild as the ascent from the Exchange to the Infirmary could be transported into the locality, it would doubtless be regarded by the natives with awe . . . If there is another noticeable feature about this place it is the disagreeable but universal appearance of newness. Every building gives an impression of having been erected about three weeks ago, and of being not yet properly dry. The houses . . . are all glaringly red, and smell of mortar, paint and paper The shrubs and trees of the garden are youthful, not to say infantile, in growth and development, and mostly useless for purposes of shade and ornament. It seems impossible to escape from the observation of smoking and hideous brick-kilns, and half-finished houses, with building materials scattered all about. There are houses of every size, shape, solidity and denomination, and it is peculiar to notice that with a diminution of the size and quality of a house the name becomes larger and grander . . .

Yet all the residents, and in particular the later ones, and those that have removed from Manchester, are firmly convinced that a more truly rural place does not exist. The amount of gardening which may be observed in the course of an evening's walk is truly startling. For the first year of any individual's residence he is prepared to go to any length in the satisfaction of his new delight. He . . . leaves his bed at unearthly hours in the morning. Then he boasts diligently and loudly all day in town on the subject . . . Wives and daughters, however, are equally enthusiastic. Watering the garden is their especial forte. This operation they carry on at all costs, and in every description of weather . . . the mania is only a passing one and rarely survives a second year's residence . . . Sale is happy in the possession of a rather greater average than usual of the young gentlemen who are known . . . as fast. They are precisely the same sort of young people, and do precisely the same sort of thing, as other fast people all over the world. They smoke bad cigars . . . and dress as brilliantly as their incomes will fairly allow. On Saturday evenings they adjourn to the Moorfield Gardens. There to the strains of a noisy . . . band . . . they indulge in those performances which constitute what is, in their phraseology, a "lark" . . . The roads of Brooklands are the same dreary appearance, beautified in many cases by the genius and capital of the late Mr. Brooks . . .'

The magazine article betrays a certain amount of waspishness in a level of humour which, though not particularly high, was fashionable in that period. The ingratiating tones regarding the "late Mr. Brooks" are obviously born of a desire not to offend his son, William Cunliffe Brooks, a powerful figure in the Manchester area. Possibly the author did not himself live in Sale and was irritated by boring accounts of life here by those who did.

The reference to "finger [sign] posts giving . . . the exact number of yards to the station" may have been prompted by his overhearing arguments between some of these new Sale residents as to who lived nearest to the railway station. The roads being "stretches of macadam and parapet" would be an accurate enough observation. Wilfred R. Burke, writing his memoirs as a boy in Sale in the 1880s, mentions Egerton Street and School Road as being the only roads in Sale which were paved and flagged throughout; the roads where better-class property had been built merely being surfaced with shale.

The "parapets" were, of course, the boundary walls between gardens and roads, built from brick and faced with sandstone blocks. This type of wall was ubiquitous in the Victorian suburbs to the south of Manchester. The comment on the brick-kilns can be dismissed as most of the villas are built from machine-made bricks, with high-quality ones used for front and side walls and inferior but still machine-made bricks at the rear.

An exception is to be found in the case of Olive Grove, now numbers 76 to 82 Northenden Road, a terrace of smaller houses built about 1860; here the rear and side walls are constructed of hand-made bricks manufactured from the local boulder clay deposited when the glaciers melted at the end of the last Ice Age about 15,000 years ago. The pebbles contained in the boulder clay can be seen in some of the bricks. The front wall is built of machine-made bricks in Flemish bond with stone quoins at the

Plate 19: The most outstanding person to reside in Sale, and one whose name is known internationally, was James Prescott Joule, F.R.S. (1818-89) who lived for the last seventeen years of his life at this house, *Rutland* 12 Wardle Road; the unit of energy called the joule being determined by him. Many of his experiments were carried out in this house which he owned and which he shared with his unmarried sister and his artist son. After his death his notebooks were discovered in the cellars. A memorial tablet to Joule was placed in Westminster Abbey directly beneath Darwin's memorial and a fund was launched locally to erect a memorial tower in Sale (now Worthington) Park, but only £300 was raised in 1902, with scientists in the U.S.A. and Germany contributing £115; the result being that the Joule Memorial, seen in Plate 20, was unveiled in Sale Park by Sir William H. Bailey in 1905.

Plate 20: The Joule Memorial

angles as high as a string-course below the first-floor windows; the front and side walls were rendered in 1975, when the windows were "Georganised". Olive Grove was built by Luke Winstanley, a builder and brickmaker, who lived in Craven Terrace; his brick-yard was situated on the north side of Dane Road in what is now the Danefield Road area.

Many of the villas are decorated with courses of brick of a contrasting colour, as are some of the window-heads, and etched or stained glass is sometimes used in doors and windows. Clever attempts were made to make many of the houses seem grander than they actually were; one method, often employed on a corner site, was to have a pair of semi-detached houses built in such a way that, to the casual observer, the building appeared as just one house, although the effect was often spoilt by the garden being obviously divided into two.

The intention was to provide for the middle-class of the mid-Victorian period, mansions in miniature, and the cost was kept down by the abolition of the brick tax in 1850 and the window tax the following year. Often built along with the house was a small coach-house, stable, hayloft and harness-room complete with paved stable-yard.

Surprisingly, most of the houses were rented rather than owner-occupied, sometimes several of them being owned by one person. By the late 1850s, the cost of house-building was reduced further by the mechanisation of brick production and hand-made bricks were, eventually, unable to compete in price.

In view of the magazine article mentioning the shops, it may be as well to see what kind of shops there actually were in Sale in the period. The census returns for 1871 disclose that on the Sale side of Cross Street there were, apart from such esoteric trades as a mangle repairer; two saddlers, two bakers, a butcher, plumber, milliner, bookseller, fishmonger and poulterer, tailor and draper, dressmaker and two shoemakers, and on the same side of Washway Road could be found a grocer, draper, shoemaker, confectioner, druggist, a fancy repository and the Post Office.

School Road contained a milliner, two butchers, a refreshment house, two tailors, three dressmakers, two greengrocers, three plumbers, three shoemakers, a tailor and dressmaker, ironmonger, two hairdressers, an estate agent, three tailors and drapers, provision dealer, two grocers and a confectioner. In addition, the Co-operative Society rented premises in School Road from 1869.

Most of the shops will have appeared after the 1850s; the population of Sale more than tripled between 1851 and 1871 from 1,720 to 5,573; Ashton also showed a marked increase, the population doubling during the same period from 1,174 to 2,359. It should be borne in mind that the population increase was to a large extent composed of people who had a large purchasing power, as indicated by the increase in the rateable value of property in Sale between the years 1841 and 1871 from £5,954 to £34,652; Ashton's rateable value increasing from £3,743 to £15,998 in the same

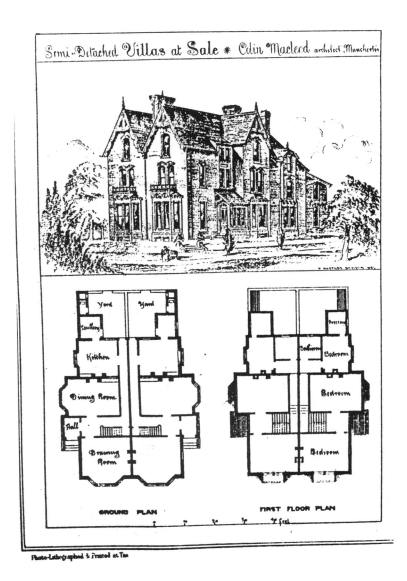

Semi-Detached Villas at Sale * Edin Macleod architect Manchester

GROUND PLAN
FIRST FLOOR PLAN

Plate 21: This sketch and plan of 1877 shows nos. 23 and 25 Irlam Road. The sketch has been based on the architect's plans and the houses, which still exist, did not turn out to be quite as grand as the illustration suggests. They are an example of a pair of semi-detached houses built to resemble one detached house, by Hughes and Co. of Openshaw, Manchester; the cost of building being estimated at £1,000 for the pair. In the report on the houses, Sale was described as "a favourite residential place of the merchants &c. of Manchester".

Plate 22: The Classical style of the 18th century in domestic architecture which Ashton New Hall reflects, was followed nationally by examples of Regency "Gothick", largely in the form of ornate "cottages" for the wealthy often having windows with pointed arches and thatched roofs in an attempt to recapture the supposed romantic life of the Middle Ages. The real Gothic Revival came later, in Victoria's reign, when many fine buildings of stone were erected, an outstanding example being Manchester's second Town Hall designed by Alfred Waterhouse.

The style was often interpreted in brick and influenced domestic architecture. *Raglan House* in Sale shown here, built in 1858 and one-time home of John Brogden, is one such example with its "medieval" doorway and porch, gables with decorative barge boards and several almost lancet windows. The entrance even has "Gothic" gateposts.

Plate 23: The "mansion in minature" provided by architects for that section of the Victorian middle-class whose ambition exceeded its wealth is illustrated perfectly by this villa of modest size, *Oak House,* at the corner of Cross Street and Atkinson Road, with its Classical porch incorporating columns with acanthus leaf decoration on the capitals in the approved manner of the Corinthian order; and, concealed by them, a pair of pilasters similarly decorated, flanking the former doorway with its elaborate rusticated work. The entrance was intended to impress and succeeds in doing so. To complete the effect the eaves cornice is crowned with a central pediment, while the brickwork is in Flemish bond and rests on a stone plinth.

A later ground-floor extension on the left interrupts the vertical line of quoins on that side and spoils the balance of the facade, for an essential characteristic of the Classical house is its symmetrical appearance. Compare *Oak House* with the seemingly careless, almost chaotic, asymmetry seen on the photograph of the Gothic style *Raglan House*, yet each has been carefully planned to conform to its particular style.

Plate 24: From about 1860 a new fashion in English architecture emerged, the Vernacular Revival, which resurrected the traditional English styles of the post-medieval period. Houses and other buildings began to appear, built from stone or brick with mullioned windows and steeply pitched roofs, reminiscent of the Elizabethan and Jacobean period.

Lloyds Bank in School Road, built in 1902, is a pleasing example of the style, being built from sandstone and brick. It has windows with splayed mullions and the bricks are thinner than the standard modern brick to be in keeping with the period the building seeks to emulate.

years. In 1879, the *Warrington Guardian* considered it worth their while launching the *Sale and Stretford Guardian* with the population of Sale at about 7,000.

The increasing affluence in Sale in the second half of the 19th century attracted the attention of the banking companies; in 1874 Parr's Banking Co. was the first to arrive, renting a house and shop in School Road at the corner of Hereford Street. This was followed in 1880 by William Cunliffe Brooks who also rented a house and shop. By the 1890s there were three banks in School Road, Parr's at no. 45; Cunliffe Brooks at no. 20 and the Manchester and County Bank at no. 8.

By 1900 Cunliffe Brooks had amalgamated with Lloyds, remaining at no. 20 until 1902 when the present Lloyds Bank building was erected at the corner of Tatton Road; Parr's Bank then moved to the vacated site (now the National Westminster at the corner of Curzon Road). In 1898 a branch of the Mercantile Bank of Lancashire was established on Northenden Road at the eastern corner of Perseverance Street (now Conway Road); this bank did not exist for very long in Sale and had gone by 1904.

At the end of the first decade of this century the banks operating in Sale were the Lancashire and Yorkshire Bank, 17 Northenden Road; Lloyds, Manchester and County, and Parr's all in School Road and the Union Bank of Manchester at 226 Marsland Road.

As already stated, the occupants of the villas were mainly merchants with businesses in or near Manchester although very few of them, or their domestic staff, were born in this part of the country. In some cases the census returns show that some of the children were born in Manchester, indicating that the family had moved from there to Sale. It is possible that some of the younger female domestic staff were obtained from the Manchester Certified Industrial School, on Northenden Road, which opened in 1877.

Certified Industrial Schools were established in several large towns during the 19th century and admitted three categories of unconvicted children under the age of fourteen belonging to the "ragged-class", the children being sent there by magistrates. These were, children found begging or wandering without visible means of subsistence; those whose parents were dead or in prison and those who frequented the company of reputed thieves.

The first Manchester Certified Industrial School was opened at Ardwick in 1846 for boys and girls. This was followed by another at Heaton Mersey in 1871 for boys only. At Ardwick, in addition to school instruction the majority of the boys were engaged in industrial employment, others were taught trades including printing; the girls were taught washing, sewing and knitting.

The report for the year 1874 states "One matter is pressing itself on the attention of your Committee, and that is, the growing necessity there is for a separate school for girls, at a distance from the present schools, and under separate management . . . at Ardwick . . . it has been found extremely difficult . . . to keep boys and girls totally apart . . . The consequence is, there has been . . . a great deal of anxiety . . .".

Plate 25: The Vernacular Revival also produced the ancestor of Stockbroker Tudor; houses built with decorative applied timber on the external walls to give the appearance of timber-framing. Many of the "half-timbered" houses in Chester were built after 1860 and deceive not only tourists into believing they are of venerable age but, apparently, others also. A work on architecture published in recent years includes a photograph of a Vernacular Revival house in Chester, the caption implying that the building is, in fact, 17th century.

The houses shown here, in Broad Road, Sale, date from 1877; the external decoration is moulded plaster rather than applied timber and the houses have ornate plaster ceilings, suggesting the ceilings of the great houses of the Tudor period in miniature.

In 1875, R. C. Browne Clayton of Chorley offered land at Sale Moor as a gift to the Institute; this was part of a field called Bottom High Field which bordered Northenden Road near the Northenden boundary and had formed part of the estate of John White, grandson of Charles White and passed through marriage to Major-General Robert Browne Clayton, father of the donor. The gift of land was accepted and plans to build the Institute went ahead, the foundation stone being laid on June 15, 1876.

The following year the building was completed and passed by H.M. Inspector of Industrial Schools. On July 4, 1877 Manchester Certified Industrial Schools' Girls Branch was opened at Sale with 72 girls transferred from Ardwick. The report of 1878 observed "there is a change for the better in the personal appearance and conduct of the girls since their removal to Sale".

The girls' day began at 6.00a.m. when they were wakened and had a period of industrial work from 6.30 to 8.00; an hour was taken up from 8.00 to 9.00 with an inspection, followed by breakfast and "family worship". The weekday breakfast consisted of ¾ pint (426 ml) of oatmeal porridge, milk and 4 oz. (113 g) bread. School and industrial work occupied the period from 9.30 to 12.00, with dinner and play during the two hours until 2.00p.m., dinner being a diet of one pint (568 ml) of rice, milk, fruit if in season or baked batter pudding with plums, made with milk; bread could be eaten in any amount. The period from 2.00 to 5.00 was taken up with school and industrial work, followed by tea and play from 5.00 to 6.30. Tea consisted of 6 oz. (170 g) of bread and treacle and a half-pint of coffee; attendance at classes occupied the period from 6.30 to 7.30, being followed by family worship until 8.00 p.m. when the girls retired to bed. The menu quoted is the one for Monday; it varied from day to day, the total consumption of meat per week being one pound (453 g) per head and other variations included suet pudding, vegetables, soup, dripping and cocoa.

Saturday morning was taken up with industrial work, followed by a walk in the afternoon and bathing, etc. in the evening. On Sunday the girls rose at 7.00a.m. with an inspection, breakfast and family worship until 9.00. The period from 9.30 to 1.00 is described as "prepare to go to place of worship", followed by dinner, 1.00 to 1.30, with reading and conversation from 1.30 to 3.00, bible class 3.00 to 4.00 and reading and conversation from 4.00 to 4.45, the half-hour until 5.15 being taken up with tea. From 5.15 the girls either prepared to go to a place of worship or attended a service in the schoolroom.

In the first year of the Industrial School at Sale, in addition to the girls transferred from Ardwick, sixteen were committed who had been found wandering without proper home or guardianship and keeping company with thieves; five had been charged with theft and one was committed as incorrigible. Their ages varied from under nine to under fourteen; four could neither read nor write; ten could read and write "indifferently", while eight could read and write "tolerably". Of these 22 girls,

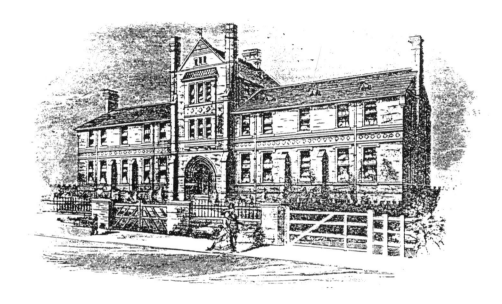

Plate 26: By the 1870s, when the Industrial School was built, most architects were using combinations of styles in the same building depending on their particular preference.

This view of the school shows the building as it was when it opened in 1877 with features representative of several periods. The Gothic Revival doorway is borrowed from the 13th century and gives entrance to a porch reminiscent of the 16th century.

In the wings, sash windows with labels suggest the late 17th century, while the buttresses dividing them take us back once again to the Middle Ages.

The south-east wing was later extended and, like the first phase, was constructed of brick in Old English bond.

one was an orphan, five had no father, three no mother and the remaining 13 had both parents living. The girls committed to the Institution were divided into two sections which alternated between attending school and engaging in work. They made their own clothes and, when work could be obtained, took orders from customers. By 1881, an examination showed most of the girls to be quite proficient in reading and writing, but the older ones to be weak at arithmetic. The report for 1881 includes the findings of an Assistant Inspector who states:

'I have visited the School this day, and examined the Children in the Schoolroom.
I find the house in good order, thoroughly clean, and well arranged.
I have not visited the School since its establishment, and am gratified by finding so good a house and such excellent accommodation.
I understand that some alterations and improvements are in contemplation. I think the large bedrooms would be made more suitable for girls by raising a partition of about 5 ft. 6 in. (slightly less than 2 metres) high right down the centre. I entirely disapprove of the dark cells in the basement, and recommend that they be not used.
I am glad to find the Children in good order. They have behaved well. I am pleased with the present aspect of the School. The girls have passed a favourable examination; they all look clean and well.'

The report for 1881 states that the average number of girls admitted that year was 102 and this is confirmed by the census return for the same year which discloses that their places of birth ranged from Scotland through many English counties to America; and that the resident staff comprised a female superintendent, house matron, school mistress, general assistant, sewing mistress, kitchen matron, laundress and a dressmaker.

Each year a number of girls were placed in service and it is quite likely that some of these were engaged locally, particularly as there was an active "ladies' committee" which solicited gifts of money, etc. to aid in the upkeep of the school. The school remained in use until 1981 and was demolished in 1985.

It will be remembered that the magazine article referred to earlier mentioned the Moorfield Gardens; this place of entertainment and athleticism was, in effect, Sale's mid-Victorian leisure centre and continued as such almost to the end of Victoria's reign; the Sale Hotel eventually being built as an addition to the complex. Another magazine article, this time describing the Gardens, appeared in 1868, entitled *At the Moorfield Gardens:*

'Sale, or possibly Brooklands, for we are not in a position accurately to distinguish the two, boasts a place of popular resort, Moorfield Gardens, with attractions somewhat resembling and probably meant to rival those of Belle Vue and Pomona Gardens. The originator and the late proprietor was a Manchester tradesman, and was generally reputed to have displayed rather a large share of eccentricity in many of his actions. Historical legends declare the establishment of the Gardens to have been due not so much to a desire for profitable investment as for the

satisfaction of personal pique and, as far as in him lay, to disgust and annoy all who considered themselves his superiors in gentility or respectability. Whether this account is correct or not, it is certain that he succeeded in planting a thorn in the flesh of most of the highly moral inhabitants of the neighbourhood . . .'

The article goes on to say that local people successfully opposed the granting of a spirit licence for the Gardens and then continues:

'The Gardens are not very extensive. Many of the striking features of their town rivals are absent. There is no boating. The wild animals and fireworks are only conspicuous by their absence. The distance from town, and the impossibility of remaining very late without considerable inconvenience, will probably have some effect on their popularity. But they possess at least one attraction, which such places as the Pomona Gardens can only attain very imperfectly, that is, a bone fide rusticity. The trees and shrubs are abundant and luxuriant, and the flowers are carefully tended and beautiful. The walks are as picturesque as the nature of the locality will admit, and the grass is as near an approach to its ancient colour as can be reasonably expected. Four days and nights out of the six the place is as quiet and deserted as its worst enemy could wish. The only visitors are an occasional lonely wedding party, whose members disport themselves on green mounds, make themselves unwell by swinging, or endeavour to keep themselves cheerful by singing plaintive melodies, and a few genteel residents who are anxious to see the Gardens, and are at least equally anxious not to be seen therein...

Certain days of the week are devoted to proceedings much more lively and exhilarating. Then music and the dance assert their sway. The place in which these amusements are indulged in presents from the outside the apearance of a barn. Within it is a large well-lighted room, with walls adorned with the usual mirrors and paintings. At one end is a refreshment bar, to which frequent recourse is rendered necessary by the violence of the exercise and the heat of the season. At the other end is the orchestra, a sort of circular cave with a highly exciting forest back-ground. Connected with, and within hearing distance of the room, is an open-air platform, where in the afternoon and early evening the dancing takes place. Of all the features in the amusements, the most unmistakable, that which it is least possible to overlook, is the music. The musicians look like working gardeners in their best clothes. Their hair is plastered down till their faces seem oily and sleek. They have evidently taken to their art from love of it, and are in the most palpable sense self-made musicians . . .

The visitors to the place (mostly) come from Manchester. But there is a large sprinkling of local people, chiefly servant maids and specimens of those who are known by courtesy as young gentlemen . . .'

Moorfield Gardens appear to have been established in 1866 when, in the Sale Rate Book for that year, their rateable value is first assessed. The property was owned and occupied by Jacob Bradford and consisted of a "house, building and greenhouse, land, refreshment rooms, pleasure grounds and building", and was known as Moor field. The previous year he is listed as owning and occupying a house, buildings and gardens

Plate 27: The Sale Hotel, originally the Moorfield Hotel, with its tower complete with parapetted observation spire and weather-vane, was built about 1879 and is the only feature of the Botanical Gardens still remaining. Most of the mahogony and etched and incised glass interior fittings were removed in the 1960s. More recently the name has been changed to the Sale Tavern and the interior rendered completely unrecognizable, while outside, the lower half of the facade is painted maroon and white which is unfortunate overlooking as it does, the pleasant Walkden Gardens opposite.

in Marsland Lane. The 1861 census discloses that the house was Moorfield Cottage and that Bradford was a toy dealer, born at Stockport.

Jacob Bradford must have died in 1867, as the rate book of October of that year names the owner of the property as the executors of the late J. Bradford and the occupier as his widow. The widow, Jane Bradford, continued to own and occupy the property, named as Moorfield Gardens in the 1869 Rate Book, until 1877 when the owner and occupier was named as Edward Bradford.

The 1871 census lists the family at Moorfield Gardens as Jane, widow, aged 56; Elizabeth Gaskell, married daughter, aged 34; Jacob Bradford, unmarried son, aged 20; Mary Bradford, daughter, aged 18 and a granddaughter and grandson, Edith and Charles Gaskell. There is no mention of an Edward Bradford, he was possibly married and living elsewhere at that time.

Edward Bradford did not remain the owner of Moorfield Gardens for very long as, although the Rate Book of May, 1877, shows him to be the owner and occupier, the name of Marmaduke Witty is written in red ink against the entry and in the Rate Book of May, 1878, John Witty appears as the owner, and Marmaduke as the occupier, of Moorfield Gardens. In the 1881 census Marmaduke Witty is described as a cotton-goods merchant, born in Manchester.

By May, 1879, a hotel later known as the Sale Hotel was added to the complex replacing Moorfield Cottage; the property now comprising a "hotel, buildings and greenhouse, land and refreshment rooms and buildings" and the following year Marmaduke Witty both owned and occupied the site which, by 1885, was called Moorfield Hotel. By 1889, the Rate Books named the site as Sale Botanical Gardens, although the name had been in general use for some years before then and continued to be the name by which the Gardens were known for the remainder of their existence. They probably closed in 1897 as the rateable value was reduced on application that year. The previous year the property had passed into the ownership of "Kay and Taylor". About 1904, the houses in Rowan Avenue, Arran Avenue, Braddan Avenue and Sylvan Avenue were built on the site.

A large-scale plan of the Botanical Gardens, drawn after 1879 when the hotel had been built and the complex was at its zenith, shows that it provided a wide number of diversions possessing, among other things, a lawn tennis and croquet ground containing a fountain and having wide herbaceous borders, an orchard and gardens containing a greenhouse about 100ft. (30.5 metres) in length; these gardens incorporated a men's and a women's open-air gymnasium.

North of the tennis and croquet ground was a bowling green and to the south of it a roughly circular lake with a mean diameter of about 100 yards (91 metres). The lake had an island containing a bandstand, being accessible by means of two bridges; to the south of it was a "rustic castle". There was also a fernery and tea room as well as a paddock and stables. Near the entrance to the gardens there was a vinery and by 1896 a cycle track and "shooting in the jungle" had been added.

The plan shows the notorious ballroom situated in the angle now formed by Cromer Road and Cumberland Road and an inset contains a recognisable drawing of the Sale Hotel with its observation tower, the only feature remaining to remind us that here, 120 years ago, was founded Sale's first leisure centre.

Although there was a great deal of opposition, locally, to the Gardens they did have their supporters and a magazine article published in 1882, headed "Sale Botanical Society" states the society "now ranks as one of the best in the north of England. The place of meeting is the Botanical Gardens and the owner of these delightful grounds gives the members of the society every facility for conducting their researches". The article goes on to say "The only drawback we know seems to be the want of a permanent licence. At a place of such respectability the only wonder is that the magistrates have not granted one before". The article continues by remarking that

Sale Hotel & Botanical Gardens.

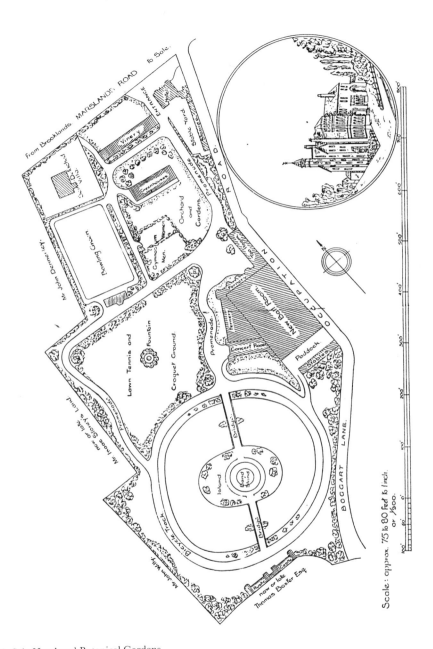

Fig 6: Sale Hotel and Botanical Gardens

the previous Saturday upwards of 300 Oddfellows from Hyde and district had a picnic at the Gardens and a special licence had to be obtained before refreshments could be served in the ballroom. It finishes by noting that "Next Saturday some grand athletic sports will be held at the Gardens, and a large amount of money will be given in prizes".

However, local memories were long and, when an application was made at Altrincham Licensing Sessions for a public music licence for the Sale Hotel, it was refused. Two property owners attended and each made a formal objection; one of them saying "When the licence was held previously it was an intolerable nuisance. The lowest class of people used to come out from Manchester to the gardens". This was said in 1935, nearly forty years after the Gardens had closed.

Another example of commercial enterprise in entertainment in the Victorian period was a skating rink and lawn for croquet and tennis which opened in 1876 and was situated "in Ashton-on-Mersey . . . within a few minutes' walk of Sale Railway Station". This appears to be distinct from a later roller-skating rink which existed early in the present century and was situated in Ashton Lane in what had been a public hall, with Ashton Council Offices at the front. Later this building was used as a variety theatre and afterwards became the Palace, Sale's first cinema, during World War 1.

In an earlier chapter mention was made of inns and public-houses which appeared in Sale during the 18th century to attract custom from the increasing wheeled traffic on the roads, most of these being situated on the main road. After the opening of the railway other public-houses came into existence to meet the needs both of the indigenous rural population and the working-class population moving into Sale as a result of the growing urbanisation of the area and the employment which this change provided in the building and servicing trades and occupations.

Most of the public-houses belonging to this period were built or converted by 1861 and, although the Vine Inn bears the date 1909, the establishment dates from the 1850s, the Rate Book of 1858 listing a beerhouse and shop at New Chester as the surrounding area was called, 1909 being the date the building was altered. The Carters Arms also existed in 1858, being named in the 1861 Census as the Jolly Carter Beer House, as did the Bridge Inn listed as a beerhouse at White's Bridge. The Queen's Hotel appears to date from 1860 and the same year a shop was added to a house at the corner of Wythenshawe Road and Northenden Road, the house changing to a public-house, named as the Nag's Head in the 1861 Census.

Property deeds show that the Railway Inn originated in 1861 as a beerhouse and shop; the Old Brooklands also originated in the 1860s. The Legh Arms dates from about 1842, the licensee at that time being Thomas Brickell who combined the occupations of innkeeper and wheelwright.

A further Victorian public-house in Sale called the Pear Tree Inn is shown on the 6 inch edition of the 1876 Ordnance Survey map, situated between what are now Symons Road and Sefton Road. Some of these public-houses had a bowling club, the

Queen's Hotel possessing a very fine green, but the only public-house bowling green now remaining in Sale is the one at the Legh Arms.

Sale's Victorian middle-class had its own diversions; as early as 1870 a report appeared in a humorous and critical journal (its own description) of the formation of the Sale Amateur Dramatic Club founded the previous year, which dealt with its first performance at the Sale Institute, originally the early 19th century Congregational Chapel, on the site of the present Town Hall.

The author of the article was rather scathing about the venue, describing the approach to the building as "rather unpleasant . . . intensely dark, dangerously steep and hopelessly dirty" the stage was "sufficiently broad, though somewhat wanting in depth"; he then observed that perhaps the "absence of stage room was not an unmitigated evil. We were thus saved from the many stiff and often meaningless struttings with which dialogue is interspersed on large stages". Among the audience were "several celebrities from other dramatic societies in the neighbourhood including the leading comedian of the Athenaeum Society". The performance, opening with a prologue, was followed by "The Babes in the Wood" and concluded with "Lend Me Five Shillings".

A later company was the Brooklands Amateur Thespian Society which started in 1893 and confined its attention to light opera. In 1877, the Sale Amateur Minstrels was formed from members of Sale Cricket Club, the purpose being to give concerts in aid of the Club funds; two years later the name was changed to the Minnehaha Amateur Minstrels, the troupe surviving until World War 2.

In 1894, the Sale Literary Society was formed as a discussion group and, later, lectures were introduced as the Society's main activity as well as excursions to places of historical interest. The Sale and District Musical Society was founded in 1907 by Alfred Higson as a competitive choir and eventually became internationally renowned both through radio broadcasts and many successes at the International Eisteddfod at Llangollen.

There were also sporting and other activities; in 1854, only five years after the opening of the railway, the Sale Cricket and Quoits Club was formed in a field near Broad Road. In 1879, the Club introduced lawn tennis. A hockey section was run separately from 1888 and continued to be for many years. Cricket and lawn tennis clubs were later formed at Brooklands and Sale Moor, Ashton having separate cricket and tennis clubs. Hunting also took place apparently, as the 1876 Ordnance Survey map shows a group of buildings on the north side of Dane Road as Sale Moor Hunting Establishment in an area now occupied by Lynn Avenue.

What was to become one of the premier Rugby Union clubs in the country was formed by members of Sale Cricket Club in 1861 and was named simply Sale Football Club; for, after all, if you lived in a place like Sale in those days, what other kind of football existed apart from rugby football? Sale joined the Rugby Union on its formation ten years later and remained a member of it when many other north-west clubs joined the Northern Union, later the Rugby League, on its formation in 1895. Even in its early years Sale was a successful club and, in the 1911–12 season, Sale won all their matches.

The first Sale Harriers were in existence in the 1890s, but it appears that the club became defunct and the present club bearing the same name was officially founded in the Temperance Rooms, later part of Gordon Stewart Motors, Cross Street, on September 7, 1911. The Harriers' headquarters were at Sale baths; an Ordnance Survey map of Sale, 1911 edition, has marked on it in red ink the course of one of their training runs in those early days, a mainly cross-country circuit of six or seven miles taking in part of Northenden and finishing at Sale Baths. Today, of course, Sale Harriers is one of the leading athletics clubs in the country. A Sale Gymnastic Club existed at the beginning of this century and probably earlier; its origin may have been the gymnasium at the Botanical Gardens.

On April 21, 1913, a public meeting at the Brooklands Hotel launched Sale Golf Club which bought the land for the course and the Regency house, one-time home of the Worthingtons, which is still the clubhouse, and the club soon had the reputation of being one of the finest in north Cheshire.

The Brooklands Hotel, at which the golf club meeting took place, was built in 1872 and was for many years a residential hotel; it was owned by the Grand Hotel in

Plate 28: The bricked-up former access to a privy in the wall of the rear garden of *Moor Lea* , Derbyshire Road, one of a group of houses built for John Morley in Holly Bank about 1857; Morley occupied the house, hence the name. Derbyshire Road at that period was known as Morley Lane. The passage-way which gave the night-soil cart access to the privy still exists.

Plate 29: The house shown here is on the opposite corner; in his memoirs Wilfred R. Burke, writing in 1945 states "even those houses that were covered all over with ivy have been stripped..." This house still retains that feature; the bay window was added early this century. The house is deceptive, it is actually one of a pair of semi-detached, the other "half" being hidden round the corner in Holly Bank and presenting a similar appearance.

Manchester and used by them as an annexe. It was there that in 1893 the Brooklands Agreement was signed at a meeting between the Federation of Master Cotton Spinners Associations and the Operative Cotton Spinners. The employers had, the previous year, announced their intention of imposing a 5% reduction in wages; this led to a strike which lasted five months, or a lock-out as the operatives claimed it was. The dispute ended with a compromise wage reduction of 2½%. The Brooklands Agreement provided for, among other things, the setting up of a tribunal of employers and workers in the cotton industry to adjudicate on disputes and was described as "the first and greatest and, indeed, the model of all treaties between capital and labour".

The hotel was purchased by Chesters Brewery in 1934 and, after lasting for a century, was demolished in 1972 to make way for an office block. A separate part of the hotel called the Brooklands Tap was retained and renamed the Brooklands Tavern.

In the latter part of the 19th century, as the population increased, the need for various essential services arose. Until the 1870s, apart from Brooks's Drain there was no sewer system in Sale, just dry lavatories, or "privies" usually situated at the far end of rear gardens or, in the case of smaller houses, backyards; these were emptied by the "night-soil" men, access usually being obtained through an aperture set in a wall and covered by wooden doors. According to the Charter Inquiry Evidence, Sale was first sewered between 1875 and 1880, although it should be noted that a cast-iron manhole cover set in the footpath at the north end of Conway Road bears the inscription "Sale Sewers 1873". Water was supplied by the North Cheshire Water Company and gas by Stretford gasworks; as late as 1934, 379 of the street lamps in Sale were illuminated by gas.

Sir W. H. Bailey, who came to live at Sale Old Hall towards the end of the 19th century, had quite a high reputation among the engineering fraternity in Manchester and Salford. However, at a meeting of the Manchester Association of Engineers in 1879, he was rash enough to say that he considered Mr. Edison's invention was about the clumsiest method of obtaining a light and that Mr. Edison should be ashamed of himself for kicking up such a fuss about nothing. Perhaps the fact that Bailey's own firm manufactured gas fittings clouded his judgment; however, the electric light has survived for more than a century.

Plate 30: Opposite to Holly Bank and now forming part of Prince's Road was Harperhill which, along with Holly Bank, comprised a small example of early Victorian landscaped roads. Some of the original trees are still there including holly trees in Holly Bank. Both Harperhill and Holly Bank were private roads with entrance gates but no lodge.

The photograph shows the sandstone gate-piers at the entrance to Holly Bank. The main piers still carry the remains of a pair of cast-iron gas lamps and the gates were topped with "spearheads" to judge by a fragment, still remaining, of part of one of the side-gates for pedestrians.

Plans for a generating station in Sale were considered in 1900 but, eventually, it was decided to take a bulk supply from the Trafford Power Company. There was some delay before this could be put into effect and a temporary steam station supplied power in the period 1902–3. Owing to an erratic supply from the Trafford Power Company the agreement was terminated in 1910; the Council then installed diesel driven generators and direct current was transmitted until 1921 when the council entered into an agreement with Manchester Corporation for a bulk supply A.C. system.

Ashton's electricity was supplied by the Altrincham Electric Supply Ltd. The Company started to supply Ashton in 1896 and also Timperley and Altrincham. Sale declined to take part, deciding to keep control in the hands of the Council. By 1929 the Altrincham undertaking supply was 150% dearer than that of Sale, which was the cheapest in the country with the exception of Hamilton. Sale District Council bought out Altrincham Electric Company's interest in Ashton in 1935.

A new court-house and police station was built in Tatton Road in 1881 and opened the following year. The building consisted of a courtroom, magistrates' retiring rooms, rooms for witnesses, officers' quarters and six cells; the cost being over £2,000. In 1936, the Chief Constable of Cheshire said at a Borough Council meeting "at Sale you have what I can only describe as a pitiful police station . . . I am going to make certain proposals . . . in a very short time you will have a police station more in conformity with the importance of the Borough and its dignity". Today, half a century later, it is still in use little changed. Two years earlier the Council had declared "our library is the only thing of which we are not proud".

In 1886, a woman benefactor gave £100 "for the benefit of the poor of Sale" which was used for the establishment of a Public Free Library, opened in 1887 and housed in a room at the Township School. A purpose-built library was erected in 1891 by public subscription and was jointly administered by Sale and Ashton, the building being owned by Sale. It comprised a reading room, lending department, lecture room and librarian's room and stocked about 10,000 volumes in its early years, the building continuing in use as a library until the 1930s. The present library in Tatton Road was opened November, 1938. A branch library was established at 103 Northenden Road about 1899 but did not last long.

A poll of the inhabitants of Sale was held in 1910 in order to ascertain public opinion regarding the proposed swimming baths, 3,444 voting papers being distributed. The result was that 1,155 were found to be in favour and 766 against; following this a Baths Committee was formed. The baths were completed in 1914 with a pool measuring 75ft. (23 metres) × 30ft. (9 metres).

As Sale was developing and changing from a rural to an urban area, so was the form of local government. In an earlier chapter we saw that Sale until well into the 19th century was administered by a vestry, composed at first of all the ratepayers and later by a select vestry consisting only of the principal ratepayers. The Public Health

Plate 31: In addition to carrying mail for the Post Office on their post-cars, the tramways also had their own parcels delivery service. For this purpose special enclosed freight-cars were used and small parcels were delivered from the parcels offices to the addressees by youths pushing box-type handcarts.

The photograph shows the former Manchester Corporation Tramways Parcel Office opened in 1927 on Cross Street at the corner of Atkinson Road. The jeweller's shop now occupying the premises is enhanced by the cast-iron and glass verandah which is the former passenger shelter.

Act of 1848 authorised the establishment of local Boards of Health and, in 1867, Sale Local Board was formed. The cemetery, opened in 1862, was administered by a Burial Board and any profits were used to subsidise the rates.

Sale Local Board was the forerunner of the District Council and the members were elected by all ratepayers; a householder whose property had a rateable value of £10 received one vote with extra votes for each further £10 of rateable value so that, for example, a householder with a rateable value of £50 had five votes. In 1894, the Urban District of Sale was constituted by virtue of the Local Government Act of that year, Ashton following suit the following year; the two Urban Districts existed side by side until the amalgamation of Sale and Ashton in 1930.

In the 20th century people became increasingly mobile as the tramway system expanded. Horse-drawn trams had first appeared in Manchester in 1877 operated by the Manchester Suburban Tramways Co. In 1880 an Act dissolved the Manchester Suburban and it was incorporated in a new company called the Manchester Carriage and Tramways Co. which ran trams as far as Stretford, having stables and tramsheds next to the Old Cock Hotel where they still exist, having been occupied by several firms after they ceased to be used for their original purpose early this century.

In 1898, the Manchester City Council appointed a Tramways Committee and the first electric service ran in 1901. The Manchester Carriage and Tramways Company went out of existence in 1903 and the same year the British Electric Traction Company announced its intention of applying to Parliament for an Act to construct the North Cheshire Tramways. Their plan was to link up to the Manchester Corporation tramways at Stretford and extend the service to Sale; in this they had the support of Sale Urban District Council. The proposal was to extend the lines to continue along Cross Street and Washway Road, terminating at Urban Road. There was to be a junction on Cross Street in order to run a service to Sale Moor via Chapel Road and Tatton Road, then along Northenden Road as far as the Industrial School.

In the meantime, Altrincham District Council were supporting Manchester Corporation in a scheme called Southern Tramways to continue their service from Stretford, through Sale to Altrincham. After lengthy negotiations it was agreed that Manchester Corporation would carry out the undertaking and, in 1907, the tram service ran to Altrincham. The previous year a service ran as far as School Road, but it was not until 1912 that it was extended to Sale Moor, and then only as far as the Legh Arms.

The lines which ran through Sale were called Sale Tramway, opened in 1906, owned by Sale Council and leased to Manchester Corporation; the capital outlay costing the Council over £65,000, of which, more than £27,000 of the loan debt was still outstanding in 1934, three years after the buses had taken over. However, the Omnibus Agreement made provision for Manchester Corporation to continue the payments set out in the original tramway leases.

The tramlines to Sale Moor were just a single track along Northenden Road with a loop-line at Craven Terrace to enable one tramcar to pull into it if another was approaching in the opposite direction; Northenden Road is still wider at this point. One day, in conditions of thick fog, occurred what, with hindsight, can be described as the inevitable; in 1925, two tramcars collided head-on in Northenden Road, eight passengers sustaining injury. The tramlines in Northenden Road were removed in the period 1932–4; those in Ashfield Road surviving until the 1940s.

By the end of Edward's reign and the beginning of the tramway era, a large part of Sale had been built on with various classes of houses and, although the area remained largely middle-class in character, house-building for the wealthy was almost at an end in Sale. The motor car age made many rural areas not served by the railway accessible and, in the 20th century, the well-to-do were having houses built in places like Mere, and many a Cheshire village acquired its share of new houses designed in the style which was dubbed stockbroker's Tudor. In the 1920s and particularly the 1930s house-building in Sale was mainly undertaken by the speculative builders of cheaply priced houses for sale and, to a lesser extent Sale Council, with **municipal houses for rent.**

Sources for Chapter 9 – The Creation of Urban Sale

Census returns, 1851–81.

Ordnance Survey map, 1876.

Sale and Stretford Guardian.

Sale Township Minutes.

Sale and Ashton-on-Mersey Rate Books.

Free Lance magazine, vol. 3, 1868, pp. 167–8.

Burke, W. R. Sale in the County of Chester. Unpublished typescript in Sale Reference Library.

Sale and Stretford Guardian Year Book, 1906; 1913.

Manchester Certified Industrial Schools' annual reports.

The British Architect and Northern Engineer, vol. 8, July 13, 1877, p. 21; vol. 6, 1876, p. 346.

Sale Moor Enclosure Award, 1806–7.

Deeds of Sale Priory.

Sphinx magazine, vol. 1, August 22, 1868; vol. 3, 1870, p. 24.

Momus magazine, vol. 8, August 10, 1882, p. 184.

Sale Guide Book, 1911.

Sale Jubilee Brochure, 1960.

Manchester Guardian, May 3, 1926.

Cowen, Frank. A History of Chesters Brewery Company, 1982.

Sale Charter Inquiry Evidence, 1934.

Slater's Directories, Altrincham and Sale.

Dean, A. C. Some Episodes in the Manchester Association of Engineers, 1938.

Simpson, Mrs. G. W. Letter to Sale Guardian, May 8, 1980.

10

The Emergence of Modern Sale

During the Victorian period and after, class-divisions became more blurred. At the top of the scale offspring of the wealthiest merchants and new industrialists married into the nobility. The middle-classes were also changing as they were diluted by a new class which, although mere employees, earned a comfortable salary. Many a clerk also, considered himself to be middle-class, although he may be earning less than a skilled artisan, who, although unquestionably working-class was at the very top of that class, and commanded a wage far in excess of the semi-skilled worker until World War I, when the gap was permanently narrowed.

The war was responsible for other permanent social changes; nearly 200,000 women entered government departments and half a million took over the clerical work in private offices. They worked on public transport and 800,000 entered engineering factories. At the British Westinghouse Co. in Trafford Park (now G.E.C.) almost one-third of the labour force during World War 1 was female. These women were mainly young and unmarried and it is significant that the number of domestic servants nationally halved, never to recover. Before the war, people of quite modest means could afford to employ a domestic; the 1881 census shows that for example in Rivershill, Ashton-on-Mersey, resident domestic servants were employed by, among others, a commercial traveller, two bank cashiers, an "agent for soap" and an agent for a woollen manufacturer.

The growth of the tramways enabled clerks and artisans to move out of the cities into the suburbs where many of them rented quite comfortable new houses. As the census returns after 1881 are not yet available, this information has to be confirmed by contemporary local directories published by Slater.

The blurring of the classes created a problem for the compilers of directories. Until the end of Edward's reign Slater's directory divided the entries into two lists; one comprising "gentry, clergy and private residents" later reduced simply to "private residents" and the other classified as "alphabetical list" which consisted of those of little or no status. Problems were bound to arise, particularly when neighbours found themselves arbitrarily divided between the two lists, with the "alphabetical" ones no doubt complaining to the publisher. The result was, that from 1911 onwards, there was merely an alphabetical list in addition to the street directory.

The information in the directories is incomplete, listing only heads of households, "private residents" not disclosing their occupation and the "alphabetical list" entries sometimes listed under the anonimity of "householder". Nevertheless, most of the occupiers of the artisans' houses do give their occupation and it is apparent they were quite mixed; a row of houses could be occupied by, among others, a clerk, teacher, electrician and insurance agent.

The social structure of Sale was slowly changing as the well-to-do began to move out and be replaced by what modern sociologists would describe as social classes C1 and C2, white-collar and skilled manual workers. At an inquiry in 1929 regarding a proposal to build a theatre and cinema at Brooklands, it was said that "the character of the district was changing, many of the large houses had been turned into boarding houses or flats".

On the same site, at the corner of Brooklands Road and Framingham Road, in 1934 the firm of R. W. Willan made an application to build a row of shops to which there was opposition; a petition against being signed by 128 residents. The houses in the Framingham Road area then known as the Brooklands estate had recently been built and, in fact, there were still 20 of them unsold. The barrister representing R. W.

Plate 32: An advertisement of about 1930.

Willan said at the subsequent hearing "the revolutionary change in the last seven years from the larger to the smaller type of house would undoubtedly increase rapidly". In the end the shops were built to a design by Harold F. V. Newsome of Manchester and blended quite well with the nearby Brooklands Hotel.

The comments quoted above were made in order to further a particular argument and did not completely show the true position at the time as, during the 1920s and to a lesser degree the 1930s, as well as housing development for the salary and wage earners, a number of houses were built in Sale for people commanding a quite substantial income.

The post-World War 1 housing situation for working-class people was extremely unfavourable; the end of the war brought a rush of marriages and a consequent housing shortage. Local authorities were ordered by Addison, the President of Local Government Board and the first Minister of Health, to build houses for rent. Expense was not permitted to delay the house-building programme and, early in 1921, Addison was paying £910 for council houses which, at that time, were quite spartan affairs, often with unplastered brick walls in the kitchen. A year or so later the same houses were built for less than £400.

As early as 1919, Ashton built 58 houses in Oaklea Road; Sale followed in 1920 with eleven houses in Brindley Avenue. By 1923, Ashton's total still stood at 58 and Sale's had risen to 40; while the housing shortage nationally was estimated at over 800,000 that year. The following year it was resolved to build 24 more houses on Clarendon Crescent and Dane Road to let at a rent of 16s.3d. (81p) per week which was reduced to 14s.8d. (73p) in 1926, a year after the houses were built. By the beginning of World War 2, a total of 594 council houses had been built in Sale and Ashton.

During the 1920s the middle-class were equipping themselves with labour-saving electrical appliances and, in 1925, the chairman of the Manchester Corporation Electricity Committee opened an exhibition of electrical equipment at Sale Town Hall to introduce a system of hiring out electric fires, cooking ranges, irons, vacuum cleaners, washing machines, etc. It was possible to hire a cooking range and quick-boiling kettle for a quarterly charge of 5s.0d. (25p) which covered installation, maintenance and renewals.

Both Metropolitan-Vickers and G.E.C. had a stand at the exhibition. Among the appliances exhibited was the Thor vacuum cleaner, said to be the only all-English model sold under 12 guineas (£12.60p); its price was £7.10s. (£7.50p); the weekly wage of a skilled tradesman in engineering in 1925 was £2.6s. (£2.30p) plus any piecework bonus he might earn.

In the 1930s, the speculative builder came on the scene on a scale not equalled before or since, building, nationally, 3,000,000 houses mainly for sale. The building boom accounted for the increase in employment between 1932 and 1935; even so, although unemployment had fallen significantly it still stood at 2,000,000 in this

Plate 33: Most of the early Council houses in Britain followed a "Georgian" style on the front elevation and were loosely based on privately built "cottages" such as those designed by Alexander Harvey for Bournville village near Birmingham which was erected 1895-1904.

This, one of two pairs of Council houses in Old Hall Road built in 1931, has sash windows at the front at that late date, three panes in width as vertically sliding sash windows usually were in the 18th century. In order to provide more light for the living room the principal window has been designed with an extra fixed section on either side of the sash.

period. On the other hand many of those who were employed were buying new houses, radios, electrical equipment and furniture. It is a fact that during the 1930s the standard of living for most people was steadily rising due to falling prices achieved in the main through improved production methods.

In 1935, in Sale, more than 900 private houses were built, most of them semi-detached. The social historians usually refer to the movement of the white-collar workers to the suburbs in connection with this phenomenal building boom, and this is true so far as it goes; but a glance in a contemporary directory will show that some manual workers also were taking on mortgages for new houses.

In Conway Road, for example, although there were people with occupations such as a manager, insurance superintendent, estate agent, etc., about half of the owner-occupiers were manual workers ranging from a toolmaker and a coppersmith, both

Plate 34: An excellent example of the small semi-detached house of the 1930s is shown here. Situated in Derbyshire Road South it is part of a development known in its day as Moor Nook Park Estate, built by W.H.Matthews about 1933; the house being quite unspoiled more that 50 years later.

The Vernacular Revival influenced even houses like this as can be seen in the gable and the leaded windows. The door, on the other hand, is fashionable Art Deco and places the house firmly in the 1930s.

highly skilled trades, to a railway boiler washer. It is hardly surprising that this should be so when the cheapest houses cost less than £300, with the weekly repayments, including rates, being 11s.0d. (55p) a week. The average weekly wage of the skilled engineering worker was £3.6s.(£3.30p) in 1936, when these houses were completed.

A few years earlier semi-detached houses had been built in Sale and Ashton which were out of the reach of the manual worker. In 1930-1 houses were advertised in Hillington Road with the cheapest priced at £650; although, by 1937, it was possible to buy a "dignified detached house" in The Avenue for the same price.

Over the course of a few years from 1931, a large housing estate was built in Ashton, the Woodheys Hall estate, with houses advertised in 1933 as "the best value in town". Included were detached houses with dining room, drawing room, breakfast room, bathroom and three bedrooms and a boxroom; the latter, over the years, graduating to a fourth bedroom. These, complete with integral garage, sold for £500.

Along with these estates of houses rows of shops were often built which were called "parades". For example the row of shops on Cross Street between Chapel Road and Ashfield Road, built at the same time as the houses centred on Ashfield Road, was named Jubilee Parade, presumably to commemorate the Silver Jubilee of 1935. The shops on Marsland Road, built along with the Conway Road houses, were known as The Parade, the ones built with the Lido were, of course, the Lido Parade and the shops built to serve the Moor Nook Park estate around Derbyshire Road South were called North Parade – the only "parade" name to survive to the present day due to its being the terminus of the 113 bus service from Moston.

There were additional plans for the Woodheys Hall estate which came to nothing. In 1938, an application was made for a provisional licence for premises to be constructed in Washway Road to be called The Watling Hotel and a further hotel to be called Woodheys Hotel; neither was approved. The nearest public house was the Pelican, situated just over the boundary in Timperley; the 18th century building had been demolished a few years previously and replaced by an example of 1930s Tudor.

In 1935, Sale Council discussed the possibility of a railway station to serve the new population in Woodheys; a new station had been under consideration by the Railway Company for some time. The Council's scheme provided for the construction of an arterial road from Washway Road, opposite Woodhouse Lane, to Heyes Lane, Timperley and it was suggested that the station be built on this road. It would serve the needs of residents in Brooklands, west Timperley and the Homelands and Woodhouse estates. The station was never built, nor was the road through to Heyes Lane, a quarter-mile gap still exists between the eastern end of Eastway in Sale and the western end of Woodhouse Lane East in Timperley. Even if the station had been built it is doubtful whether it would have been used much by people on the Woodhouse estate, as between them and the proposed station lay Washway Road, which carried

Plate 35: During the 1930s younger architects attempted to design houses which reflected the age. The photograph shows a house in Cranleigh Drive, one of a row built in a style sometimes called Georgian streamline; it has a minimum of ornament and the horizontal window panes are intended to give an impression of speed, a favourite 1930s topic, with air, land and water speed records being constantly broken.

Plate 36: During the 1920s the International Modern style of architecture evolved on the Continent and later appeared in England. The house shown here is no. 267 Washway Road, originally named *Charnwood* . It is one of a group of eight houses built in the International Modern style in 1935-6 when this type of house was still rare in England.

The houses were designed by R.A. Cordingley and D.McIntyre and are typical of the style with flat roofs, rendered external walls and an abundance of steel windows in wood frames. No. 263, originally *Anlaby* was designed and built to order, the others being designed in three types and offered for sale, intended to attract small professional-class families.

These eight houses, along with no. 295 Washway Road, are the only ones in Greater Manchester included in Jeremy Gould's *Modern Houses in Britain, 1919 - 1939* .

NORTHENDEN RD. SALE MOOR.   MA.14.

Plate 37: This photograph showing Northenden Road in the early 1930s was taken near Temple Road. The approaching bus is one of those which replaced the trams on the no. 49, Sale Moor to Piccadilly route.

In the right foreground the Sale Moor sub-Post Office is shown at no. 144a, having occupied these premises from 1910 when it moved there from no. 162. The sub-Post Office has occupied its present premises at no. 133 from about 1939.

Approximate dating of the photograph is possible as the bus service commenced in 1931 and the tramlines shown here were removed by 1934.

a frequent bus service to Altrincham and Manchester operated by Manchester Corporation from 1931.

There had been a limited motor-bus service running in Sale from the 1920s, starting in 1923 with a service to Altrincham operated by John Wood and Son Ltd., this being superseded by the Altrincham District Co. which, in turn, after a few years was taken over by the North Western Road Car Co. In 1930, Sykes Bros. of Sale ran a service from Manchester, through Sale, to Hale Barns until taken over by Manchester Corporation in 1932; North Western ran a regular service at that time between Sale, Ashton and Urmston.

When the Birchfields Road car shed of Manchester Corporation Tramways was opened in 1926, the tramcar was nearing its end as the main means of public transport in the Manchester area. There had been a campaign for some years to replace the trams with buses, and it is to be supposed that the discussions had not been without rancour to judge by an extraordinary speech made by Alderman Bowes, chairman of the Tramways Committee at the ceremony of the laying of the foundation stone of the Birchfields Road depot, at which he said that the tramways had "for years been subjected to an insidious campaign of calumny, so persistent in character and unscrupulous in conduct that it could only be taken as being the outcome of an organised scheme to discredit this form of transport". The Tramways Committee at that time also operated a fleet of 58 buses which was "valued very highly in its proper sphere but is not the instrument for our busy streets . . . the reliable tramcar was still . . . the peoples' motor-car".

The main bus services in Sale replaced the tramcars in 1931 and used the same routes and route numbers. The 47 and 48 ran to Altrincham, the 47 from Piccadilly and the 48 from Exchange; in more recent years these became, respectively, the 263 and 264. The 49 service operated between Piccadilly and Sale Moor where it ran along James Street and Alice Street, terminating in Hampson Street; from 1939 alternate buses terminated at the Conway Road–Norris Road junction; later they alternated between Conway Road and Derbyshire Road South. When this service ran through to Moston it was re-numbered 112 and 113 with the termini at Helsby Road and North Parade. To be strictly accurate, there were Manchester Corporation buses running from Sale Moor to Piccadilly before the tram services were withdrawn, but these ran only during the "rush hours" in the morning and evening. The 50 bus service from Piccadilly, through Northenden to Brooklands terminating at the Vine Inn, commenced to operate during the 1930s and, eventually, became the 41 service from Exchange, terminating at Woodheys. When World War 2 started the 71 service from Wythenshawe, through Sale to Trafford Park, was introduced and, after the war, the 99 service from Piccadilly came into being, originally terminating in Dane Road at the Temple Road junction. These were the main services; there were, also, local ones which operated within the Borough boundaries.

In the period 1930–40, car-ownership nationally doubled from 1,000,000 to nearly 2,000,000 registered vehicles. The motor-car age brought a conversion from gas to electric street lighting along the main road in Sale and Ashton in the 1920s and demands for stricter speed limits in the 1930s.

It will be remembered that up to 1935 electricity in Ashton and Sale was supplied by two different undertakings. This created difficulties for a joint lighting scheme to be installed along the main road, as the boundary between the two districts ran along the centre of the main road. In 1919, Sale's Engineer prepared a plan for a joint lighting scheme, but Ashton declined to adopt it. By 1926 a Main Road Lighting sub-Committee had been set up by Sale and Ashton and, at a meeting, the Ashton representatives explained their proposal for lighting the Ashton side of the road by electricity and to obtain better pressure for the gas lamps on the Sale side. The final outcome was that Ashton refused to take part in a joint lighting system and, although the main road was lit on both sides by electric lights, Ashton installed "Blaizolite" lamps while Sale decided that "Rodalux" were more suitable.

From 1930–1934 all speed limits on the roads were abolished. At the end of this period a speed limit of 30 miles per hour in built-up areas was imposed, as was a driving test for those not already holding a driving licence; even so the number of road fatalities that year was greater than in 1964 when there were six times the number of cars in use. When the 30 m.p.h. speed limit was introduced it brought a lot of criticism. In Sale a local businessman described it as "ridiculous" and wondered whether it was worthwhile having a car for business purposes. Another driver said that the use of plain-clothes police in cars was "not cricket".

The same year waiting restrictions were proposed in School Road, which, at a Ministry of Transport inquiry at Sale Town Hall, was described by one person as "a thousand yards of terror". On the Saturday of the previous week, the number of vehicles using School Road had totalled more than 4,000 and there had been 22 accidents there in a period of about eighteen months. From all of this it can be surmised that, in the 1930s, car-ownership in Sale was probably well above the national average.

There was a firm of motor engineers on Cross Street, near Park Avenue, as early as 1906; this was the firm of Seymour and Major known, by 1908, as Seymour, Son and Foster which became Gordon Stewart Motors in 1927. A car saleroom was added the following year, the premises being demolished in 1986. By 1934, there was a total of six motor repairers, engineers and petrol stations in Sale, including the Royal Garage on both sides of Cross Street, styled at the time "the world's largest garage". The grassed forecourt was graced by two reclining stone lions which once had guarded the entrance to Trafford Hall and ended their days painted to advertise Regent petrol.

Mass entertainment expanded rapidly during the 1930s, expressed to a large extent in the building of "luxury" cinemas. The first cinema in Sale was the Palace in Ashton Lane opposite Park Road which, as stated in the previous chapter, dated back as a cinema to World War 1. Shortly afterwards the Savoy was built in Ashfield Road and underwent alterations in 1924. Undoubtedly, the most splendid cinema in Sale was the Pyramid on Washway Road; this was designed by Drury and Gomersall in an "Egyptian" style, hence the name. The Pyramid was built 1933–4 to seat 2,000 at a cost of £70,000. The building included a first-floor cafe advertised as the "rendezvous for discerning folk" and, flanking the cinema, two rows of shops were built in a style which harmonised with the nearby Post Office.

Once built the Pyramid then needed a licence to open; this was refused by the magistrates after opposition from, among others, the Palace and Savoy cinemas and the Regal, Altrincham. A protest meeting was organised by a local committee which included the vicar of St. Paul's. The meeting was a success, as the Pyramid's 2,000 seating capacity was filled and another 2,000 gathered outside; a petition had attracted 18,000 signatures.

The result was that a licence was then granted and the Pyramid was opened for its first public performance on Monday, February 26, 1934 with a film and stage show. It is a cinema typical of prosperous suburbia of the 1930s and was built with a spacious car park. The Pyramid was bought by Rank in 1941 and, later, became an Odeon cinema. The Odeon showed its last film in October 1981; the cinema was sold and later re-opened as the Tatton, finally closing in 1984.

The fourth and last cinema to be built in Sale was the Warwick on Northenden Road which opened without incident in August, 1939, having a seating capacity of 1,250. The screen was flanked by two representations of Oscar, the annual award made in Hollywood, U.S.A. for alleged achievement in the making of films.

On July 10, 1935, Sale Lido opened on Washway Road. The 130 ft. (39.6 metres) swimming pool, which was half the length again of the main pool in the modern leisure centre, could be covered and used as a dance floor; the building also possessed a domed solarium and was part of a complex which included a row of shops. During World War 2, the Lido was used as offices by Metropolitan-Vickers and was re-opened by Mecca Ltd. as the Locarno Ballroom.

It is a sobering thought that, with the exception of the Temple Inn, not a single public-house (or "hotel" to use the suburban euphemism) was built in Sale from the reign of Victoria unil the 1960s. The Old Brooklands Hotel on Marsland Road can be deceptive as it appears to be a typical example of brewer's Tudor of the 1930s, whereas it was merely altered and extended and dates from the 1860s. Locals referred to it as the little "B" in order to distinguish it from the Brooklands Hotel which they called the big "B".

As a matter of fact, no new public-houses were needed in Sale in the 'thirties for the new population, as car-owners among them could drive out to Plumley, Lymm, Peover, or similar places and relax among oak beams and copper kettles. In those days a public-house was considered to have a certain standing if it attracted a sizeable number of "car-people". Others, some of whom had deliberately chosen to leave an environment liberally sprinkled with public-houses would, accompanied for the most part by their wives, visit the Sale Hotel or the Brooklands which were pleasant enough places in those days, as were the Woodcourt and the Pelican outside the Sale boundary. The Old Brooklands was also popular, particularly with the Rugby Union fraternity.

"Cultural activities", as amateur participation in the arts is called nowadays, expanded in Sale after World War 1. Sale Operatic Society succeeded Brooklands Amateur Thespian Society and, in the 1930s, a number of amateur dramatic societies based on churches were formed. The 1940s saw the birth of more dramatic societies such as Sale Nomads, Sale Amateur Players and the Moor Nook Players, as well as Sale Symphony Orchestra, Sale Music Club and the re-forming of the Photographic Society which had lapsed during the war.

On the sporting side there were in Sale, in 1934, 86 tennis courts, 15 bowling greens excluding those attached to public-houses, eight each of cricket, rugby and soccer pitches, three putting greens, four hockey pitches and two golf courses.

Five years after the amalgamation of Ashton and Sale in 1930 as the Urban District of Sale, the District was created a Municipal Borough with a Mayor and Corporation and presented with a Charter of Incorporation in September, 1935, the first Council meeting being held on November 9. The Town Hall had been built in 1914 and later extended, the work being completed in 1939.

There was a need for more schools in Sale in the 1930s to meet the needs of the increasing number of children. Up to then the schools in Sale and Ashton under the control of Sale Education sub-Committee were St. Martin's; St. Mary Magdalene; All Saints; Barkers Lane; Sale Higher Elementary (formerly the township school); St. Anne's; Springfield; St. Joseph's and Worthington Road, erected in 1905 as the first Council School in Cheshire. There were also a number of private schools; among them, the High School for Boys, originally in Poplar Grove, which was a preparatory school for Manchester Grammar School, and became Brooklands Primary in 1949; the Grammar School for boys, Marsland Road; the High School for girls (later Sale Girls' Grammar); the Technical School, Tatton Road and the Central School, Claremont Road.

The population of Sale increased by 6,000 in three years from 32,000 in 1934 to 38,000 in 1937 and, consequently, work was urgently begun on the building of more schools. In 1938, Urban Road, Woodheys, and Park Road primary schools were built and a new grammar school for boys was opened in Moss Lane. When the war started, work had begun on three new senior schools, one at Sale Moor and two in Ashton. No more schools were built in Sale until the 1950s, beginning with Lime Tree Primary in 1951.

By 1938 plans had been made for the evacuation of children, and mothers with children under five years of age; they were to be billeted in private houses in reception areas. Sale was a neutral area so that it neither evacuated nor officially received evacuees; however, some families moved into Sale in 1939, at the outbreak of war, from evacuation areas.

Sale did suffer a certain amount of bomb damage during World War 2. In September, 1940, incendiary bombs fell in Derbyshire Road South and Hulme Road, and the following month eight high-explosive bombs were dropped, one partly-demolishing a house in Dane Road. A large crater was blasted in Ravenstone Drive and other bombs fell in Cow Lane, none of them causing casualties. In November of the same year there was an almost direct hit on Worthington Road School and some damage was caused at the Girls' Grammar School. Four people were injured when a bomb fell behind a house in Oulton Avenue.

Three days before Christmas, 1940, six bombs demolished or extensively damaged houses in Penrith Avenue, Cumberland Road and Derbyshire Road, injuring twelve people; another bomb blasted a large crater at the rugby ground in Woodbourne Road. The following day 600 incendiary bombs were dropped on Sale in a period of three hours; the first floor of Woolworths in School Road was almost destroyed and the Council Chamber at the Town Hall was gutted. The last significant air-raid on Sale was in May, 1941, when two high-explosive bombs caused extensive damage to St. Paul's Mission Hall, Dargle Road.

House-building, interrupted by the war, continued in post-war Sale with some private development, although not on the pre-war scale, and an emphasis on municipal housing starting with 100 prefabricated bungalows, begun in 1946, off Derbyshire Road South. Between 1946 and 1960 1,540 houses of various types were completed by Sale Borough Council and, in 1966, another estate was erected in the Gratrix Lane area, principally to house the tenants of the prefabricated bungalows, which were then demolished and a further small estate built on the site. In the early 1970s, Manchester City Council completed a housing estate in Ashton-on-Mersey.

In February, 1973, a sample survey was made of people shopping in Sale town centre; this was prompted by a finding made two years earlier that well below half of the total purchasing power of Sale's population was actually spent in the town; whereas in Altrincham, between 1961 and 1971 the proportion of its total purchasing power spent there rose from 69% to 89%. It was found that only 7% of the shoppers interviewed in Sale lived outside the Borough and that most of those either worked in Sale or were visiting here anyway. In one respect, perhaps the Sale traders of forty years before were vindicated by some of the shoppers, as there were complaints about having to cross the main road to reach the Post Office.

The results of the survey made the advisory plan for the Central Area of Sale, already under development, out of date; this plan was prepared by consultants in 1964. A new policy plan, therefore, was drawn up in 1973 which provided for, among other things, the retention of Central Area (School Road) shops. Saturday, March 10, 1973 was the last day on which School Road was open to normal traffic, although vehicles delivering goods to the shops still had access; it was nearly ten years after this that School Road was re-paved and completely pedestrianised.

By the late 1960s, plans were in hand to construct a new swimming pool on an adjacent site to the swimming baths built in 1914; this new pool was intended to supplement the old one. However, it was later decided to demolish the old baths and build a completely new complex covering the two sites and work commenced in 1971. When completed it consisted of a swimming pool which, at 25 metres, is two metres longer than the old one, and a training pool measuring 75ft. (23 metres) × 30ft. (9 metres), the same dimensions as the 1914 one. In addition there is a sports hall and many other amenities. The official opening was held on July 25, 1973.

In 1972 an Act was passed to re-organise local government in England and Wales, the first time this had been done since the Norman Conquest. In 1974 a Charter was granted creating the Borough of Trafford which comprised the former boroughs of

Plate 38: A view of School Road in the 1950s looking towards Sale Bridge. The garden of the Wesley Chapel is just off the photograph in the right foreground, the site now being occupied by the Mall; just beyond it can be seen Cloughs drapers and funeral directors, a business which was established there in 1872 and survived until the 1970s.

Photo courtesy of the Francis Frith Collection

Altrincham, Sale and Stretford; the new Borough officially coming into existence on April 1 of that year. At the same time the new County of Greater Manchester was created which included Trafford and had an area of 500 square miles. From the beginning the administrators of the huge conglomerate sought to create a homogeneity within its boundaries going so far as to produce a map of the "Countie of Greater Manchester" based on John Speed's 17th century county maps. Most of the inhabitants south of the Mersey, however, continued to use the correct postal address of Cheshire, and Greater Manchester lasted twelve years, being abolished on March 31, 1986.

The largest recreational facility to appear on the scene in Sale, the water park, arose through Sale Borough Council making a virtue of necessity. In 1972, work began in order to extend the M63 motorway in a south-easterly direction to join the M56. A

Plate 39: An official visit led by the Mayor of Sale, Clr. R. Mee, on October 2, 1972 to the excavation which was later to be Sale Marina. Examining the remains of the trees are, left to right; W. Norris, Chief Public Health Inspector; N.V. Swain; Ald. F.S. Laughton; Dr. I.M. Simpson; Clr. E.McPherson and W.H.P. Owen, Deputy Town Clerk.

Photo courtesy of Altrincham and Sale Guardian

flyover was constructed to carry the extension over the A56 at Stretford and the motorway embankment was continued from the flyover, along the Mersey valley, through Sale. One million cubic yards (three-quarters of a million cubic metres) of filling were needed to construct the embankment. The Ministry informed Sale Borough Council that if the material was brought from Derbyshire, this would entail a heavy vehicle passing through Sale every eight seconds. Faced with this prospect, the Council agreed that the filling could be taken from the Mersey valley, persuaded that the resulting excavation would fill with water and Sale would then have a marina.

This method of obtaining the material for the embankment must have reduced costs enormously compared to the expense of transporting it from Derbyshire, but the Ministry's gratitude was not manifested in any particular way. Initially, the excavation was to have been about half the depth it eventually reached and about three-quarters of a mile in length, which would have created a sizeable stretch of water; but instead, the marina finished up at half the proposed length and twice the depth. When all the required material was extracted the pumps were removed and the hole gradually filled with water, but only to the level of the water table which is about twenty feet (six metres) below the surface in that area. This necessitated future work being carried out using earth-moving equipment to slope the sides down to the water level.

The excavation was, I would estimate, 80 to 100ft. (24 to 30 metres) in depth, and the sheer sides revealed the strata indicating the geological development of the area from the Triassic period, 150–200 million years ago, to the present day. The oldest rock revealed was brownish-red and grey sandstone and siltstone which, when dry and hard, has a very pleasant appearance. Higher up the walls of the excavation was the boulder clay left by the melted glaciers of the last Ice Age which contained boulders and pebbles, some of which had originated in the Lake District.

The upper deposits of sand and gravel contained a large quantity of trees which Carbon–14 tests at Birmingham University showed to be about 4,000 years old; the trees were about eight metres below the surface and included pine and, possibly, oak; also found were alder and hazel seeds. A report on the remains of the trees and the geological features revealed by the excavation was given by Dr. I. M. Simpson, head of Manchester University Department of Geology, to a meeting of Sale Civic Society in September, 1973.

Very probably the Mersey valley in this area was wooded for some millenia in a period beginning some time after the end of the last Ice Age, 10,000 to 15,000 years ago, and continuing up to the Middle Ages. Several field-names in the valley in Sale include the element 'hurst' (Anglo-Saxon *hyrst* – a wood) and, flowing along the valley is Barrow Brook (A.S. *bearo broc* – brook in the wood).

Sale Marina is extensively used by families as well as anglers, wind-surfers and water-skiers. On a busy summer day ice-cream sales thrive amid the sound of radios and children. Trafford Borough Council has now completed plans to build a water-sports centre which will include a boat-house, restaurant and licensed bar at a cost of about £725,000.

It is difficult to imagine that not very long ago the area was used as a refuse tip and that centuries before, an observer in that area would have witnessed the ploughman trudging behind his ox-team and long-extinct strains of cattle grazing the pasture. The same observer could not possibly have foreseen the changes which were to take place, but I hope that this work has enabled the reader to create in his mind a picture of each successive stage of development which led, finally, to modern Sale.

Sources for Chapter 10 – The Emergence of Modern Sale

Metropolitan-Vickers Electrical Co. Ltd., 1899–1949.

Census returns, 1881.

Slater's Directories, Altrincham and Sale.

Sale and Stretford Guardian.

Manchester Evening Chronicle.

Kelly's Directories, Manchester and Suburbs.

Green, Frank. Manchester and District Old and New, 1933.

Healey, E. K. Letters to Sale Guardian. March 9, 1973; March 23, 1973.

Manchester Guardian.

Sharp, Dennis, ed. Manchester, 1969.

Sale Jubilee Brochure, 1960.

Sale Charter Inquiry Evidence, 1934.

Sale Guide Books.

Pevsner, Nikolaus, and Hubbard, Edward. **The Buildings of England. Cheshire. 1971.**

Sale Central Area Policy Plan, 1973.

APPENDIX A

Population of Sale and Ashton-on-Mersey

	1801	1811	1821	1831	1841	1851	1861	1871	1881	1891
Sale	819	901	1,049	1,104	1,309	1,720	3,031	5,573	7,916	9,644
Ashton	788	918	875	974	1,105	1,174	1,476	2,359	3,325	4,324

	1901	1911	1921	1931	1951	1961	1971	1981
Sale	12,088	15,044	16,337	28,071	43,167	51,336	55,390	57,824
Ashton	5,563	7,324	7,773					

Sale and Ashton amalgamated in 1930. Due to World War 2 there was no census in 1941.

APPENDIX B

Buildings in Sale listed as being
of architectural or historic interest

Barracks Farm; Marsh Farm; St.Martin's Church; Ashton stocks; Ashton New Hall; barn at Ashton New Farm; Buck Inn; Ashton pinfold; Brooks's Institute; St. Martin's School; 77 Harboro Road; 118-120 Cross Street; the dovecote, Rifle Road (to be moved to Walkden Gardens); Sale Golf Clubhouse; the wall at Priory Gardens.

The above information is based on the official list which is not wholly reliable as dates and descriptions given and omitted here are not always correct and the list, although divided between Ashton and Sale, gives 77 Harboro Road as being located in Sale when it is actually in Ashton; also included in Ashton is Ackers Farm, Carrington.

INDEX

Explore the countryside with Sigma!

We have a wide selection of guides to individual towns, plus outdoor activities centred on walking and cycling in the great outdoors throughout England and Wales. This is a recent selection:

Cycling . . .

CYCLE UK! The definitive guide to leisure cycling
– Les Lumsdon *(£9.95)*

OFF-BEAT CYCLING & MOUNTAIN BIKING IN THE PEAK DISTRICT
– Clive Smith *(£6.95)*

MORE OFF-BEAT CYCLING IN THE PEAK DISTRICT
– Clive Smith *(£6.95)*

50 BEST CYCLE RIDES IN CHESHIRE
– edited by Graham Beech *(£7.95)*

CYCLING IN THE COTSWOLDS
– Stephen Hill *(£6.95)*

CYCLING IN THE LAKE DISTRICT
– John Wood *(£7.95)*

CYCLING IN SOUTH WALES
– Rosemary Evans *(£7.95)*

CYCLING IN NORTH STAFFORDSHIRE
– Linda Wain *(£7.95)*

BY-WAY TRAVELS SOUTH OF LONDON
– Geoff Marshall *(£7.95)*

Walking . . .

RAMBLES IN NORTH WALES
– Roger Redfern

HERITAGE WALKS IN THE PEAK DISTRICT
– Clive Price

EAST CHESHIRE WALKS
– Graham Beech

WEST CHESHIRE WALKS
– Jen Darling

WEST PENNINE WALKS
– Mike Cresswell

NEWARK AND SHERWOOD RAMBLES
– Malcolm McKenzie

RAMBLES AROUND NOTTINGHAM & DERBY
– Keith Taylor

RAMBLES AROUND MANCHESTER
– Mike Cresswell

WESTERN LAKELAND RAMBLES
– Gordon Brown

WELSH WALKS:
Dolgellau and the Cambrian Coast
– Laurence Main and Morag Perrott

WELSH WALKS:
Aberystwyth and District
– Laurence Main and Morag Perrott

– all of these books are currently £6.95 each.

Long-distance walking . . .

THE GREATER MANCHESTER BOUNDARY WALK – Graham Phythian

THE THIRLMERE WAY – Tim Cappelli

THE FURNESS TRAIL – Tim Cappelli

THE MARCHES WAY – Les Lumsdon

– all £6.95 each

We also publish:

A fabulous series of 'Pub Walks' books for just about every popular walking area in the UK, all featuring access by public transport

**A new series of investigations into the Supernatural,
Myth and Magic**

Superb illustrated books on Manchester's football teams

– plus many more entertaining and educational books being regularly added to our list. All of our books are available from your local bookshop. In case of difficulty, or to obtain our complete catalogue, please contact:

Sigma Leisure, 1 South Oak Lane, Wilmslow, Cheshire SK9 6AR

Phone: 0625 – 531035   Fax: 0625 – 536800

ACCESS and VISA orders welcome – call our friendly sales staff or use our 24 hour Answerphone service! Most orders are despatched on the day we receive your order – you could be enjoying our books in just a couple of days.